Praise for
Hope for the Journey

"Pastor Waller communicates encouraging, practical spiritual truths about our trials, our struggles, our victories and our relationship with the Lord. Reading this book is a treat—just like hearing Alyn preach."

Dr. Craig S. Keener
Professor of New Testament
Palmer Theological Seminary of Eastern University

"This is classic Alyn Waller, bringing the power of Christian faith to bear on the nitty-gritty challenges of contemporary life. Thoroughly biblical in its approach, theologically sound in its wisdom, refreshingly colloquial in its language and luminously practical in its orientation, *Hope for the Journey* is good food for the soul!"

Rev. Willette A. Burgie-Bryant
Director of Student Formation & Seminary Chaplain
Palmer Theological Seminary of Eastern University

HOPE
FOR THE
JOURNEY

Believing God Is Enough When the Road Gets Rough

DR. ALYN E. WALLER

PUBLICATIONS

Fort Washington, PA 19034

Published by CLC Publications

U.S.A.
P.O. Box 1449, Fort Washington, PA 19034

GREAT BRITAIN
51 The Dean, Alresford, Hants SO24 9BJ

AUSTRALIA
P.O. Box 469, Kippa-Ring QLD 4021

NEW ZEALAND
118 King Street, Palmerston North 4410

Hope for the Journey
© 2011 by Alyn E. Waller
All rights reserved. Published 2011

ISBN-10 (trade paper): 1-936143-14-3
ISBN-13 (trade paper): 978-1-936143-14-6

Cover design: Davy Montgomery
Text design: E. Richard Brodhag
Discussion questions: Laura Pollard

Unless otherwise indicated, all Scripture quotations are from the Holy Bible, King James Version, 1611.

Scripture quotations marked NIV are from the Holy Bible, New International Version, © 1973, 1978, 1984 by International Bible Society. Used by permission of Zondervan Bible Publishers.

Printed in the United States of America

19 18 17 16 15 14 13 12 11   1 2 3 4 5 6

*And we know that all things work together for good
to them that love God, to them who are the called
according to his purpose.* Romans 8:28

I thank God for His help and for hope for my journey.

CONTENTS

INTRODUCTION

I tell you the truth; It is expedient for you that I go away: for if I go not away, the Comforter will not come unto you; but if I depart, I will send him unto you. John 16:7

Do you know that there is Someone who longs to encourage you, lead you in righteousness and intercede for you? When Christ ascended into heaven, He said, "I will pray the Father, and he shall give you another Comforter, that he may abide with you for ever" (John 14:16).

The Holy Spirit isn't just some abstract concept invented to comfort new believers. He's not an "it" or an impersonal force; He is an ever-present being who leads, corrects and consoles us along life's journey.

But we are not only to be led and taught by the Spirit; Ephesians 5:18 tells us to "be filled with the Spirit." In this verse the Greek verb "to be filled" is in the present perfect or active perfect tense, which means that the action continues. In other words, you aren't just filled with the Spirit once—His power and presence are renewed and refreshed again and again, and in order to lead a victorious Christian life, you need His indwelling power. If you don't learn to listen to the Spirit's direction, you won't get very far in your Christian walk.

The Holy Spirit is the third Person of the Godhead, and He wants to relate to you and guide you in all things. Will you let Him fill your life with peace, joy and hope?

You see, it's only by the power of the Holy Spirit that we can see past the messes and storms of our lives to discover our God-given purpose. Through His abiding presence, we are given hope for the journey.

1

A GREAT STORY

And when he was entered into a ship, his disciples followed him.
And, behold, there arose a great tempest in the sea, insomuch that
the ship was covered with the waves: but he was asleep. And his
disciples came to him, and awoke him, saying, LORD, *save us: we*
perish. Matthew 8:23–25

Your life is going to be a great story.

God has a plan for you that reaches far beyond your wildest understanding. He desires to lead you in a hope-filled journey toward your ultimate destiny.

Sounds good, doesn't it? That's because it is. God's plan is infinitely better than anything you could accomplish on your own. There is, however, a slight catch. Having a "great story" doesn't mean what you might think—you don't just get to coast through life to your happily ever after.

Take a moment to think about what makes a good movie, a good plot or a good life. You might note that *good* doesn't mean *easy*. Be honest: you wouldn't want to watch a film set in a utopian world. If all the characters had great childhoods, great college experiences, great lives and great funerals, there wouldn't be any room for development or growth. A film without any trials, snags or complications wouldn't fare very well at the box office.

You see, we aren't interested in sugar-coated stories. We're interested in the truth of our lives that happens somewhere in-between diapers and coffins, and it can be messy. Having a "good" life involves facing challenges!

Difficulties make our successes all the more significant. Take for instance the story of Vivien Thomas, an African-American surgical technician whose moving story was told in the film *Something the Lord Made*. Thomas was known for his deftness and sharp intellect. Despite his lack of a college education, he worked for many years at Johns Hopkins University as surgeon Alfred Blalock's assistant. In the 1940s the two men developed a procedure to treat a serious heart condition in infants. Thomas helped Blalock perform the first life-changing surgeries, thus proving the procedure's effectiveness, but racial and academic prejudices prevailed— all the praise went to Blalock.

When we watch the movie, we're brought to tears not because of the wonderful things that Thomas accomplished but because of the challenges he had to overcome. We're moved when, over thirty years after his surgical career, Thomas is finally recognized for his achievements and presented an honorary doctorate degree from Johns Hopkins. Why does this affect us? Because we know that, to have his accomplishments acknowledged, Thomas had to overcome prejudice. Success wasn't just handed to him on a silver platter, and his struggles lent value to his time of celebration.

God Uses Serious Storms to Refine Us

Do you currently feel like you're going through a storm? You're not alone. In his book *Preaching Through a Storm*, H. Beecher Hicks states that everyone is in one of three categories: in a storm, headed out of a storm, or on the way to a storm.

In Matthew 8:23–25 we read that the disciples faced a storm of their own and were frightened, despite the fact that Jesus was with them: "And when he [Jesus] was entered into a ship, his disciples followed him. And, behold, there arose a great tempest in the sea, insomuch that the ship was covered with the waves: but he was asleep. And his disciples came to him, and awoke him, saying, LORD, save us:

The disciples were obeying God's call when they found themselves in the middle of a storm.

we perish." This storm is not one that our minds can easily justify, since it occurs not when the disciples are doing something wrong but when they are following Christ.

Jonah's storm back in the Old Testament makes more sense. Unlike the disciples, Jonah was running from God. Jonah was trying to escape the work God had told him to do; therefore, when his storm comes, we're not surprised. We expect some sort of retribution for his actions.

In Matthew, however, the disciples were behaving and obeying God's call when they found themselves in the middle of a storm.

This suggests that just because you're enduring a storm doesn't mean you've been disobedient—maybe God just has something He wants you to learn.

The disciples had to learn that following Jesus wasn't going to be a walk in the park. The storm they faced immediately precedes the significant ministerial experience of Jesus healing the demon-possessed men in the graveyard of the Gadarenes. Let me repeat that: right before *major ministry*, a serious storm struck. The disciples' storm was not one that negatively impacted them but one that strengthened them for the future.

Sometimes right when God is getting ready to take us to the next level of our faith, a storm comes along.

Am I Alone in My Storm?

Have you ever felt like you're weathering the winds and waves alone? The disciples did. The mind-blowing part of their story is that when they ran to Jesus for help, He was asleep! I can imagine their shock and consternation at that moment: "We're up here fighting for our lives, and You're *sleeping*?!"

We can understand where they're coming from because we too, at some point in our lives, have asked, "Lord, how could You be asleep in the midst of my storm?"

> *Jesus was in control of their storm, and He's on top of your situation as well.*

You're praying, but you aren't hearing anything in return. You're tithing and doing all the right things, but God feels distant. Are you wondering if God has turned His back on you—or worse, fallen asleep?

The disciples did the same thing. They saw that Jesus was resting and cried out, "Lord, save us!" Jesus was in control of their storm, and He's on top of your situation as well. You might be a little concerned by the wind and waves, but Jesus—mighty in power—isn't bothered by physical problems. In the middle of the storm, He's so chill He's sleeping.

Now, I've been quoting from Matthew, but in the other Gospels, when the disciples find Jesus resting, they're a bit more indignant and accusatory. In Mark, for example, they barge in on Jesus who's trying to get a little shuteye and shout, "Don't You even care that we are about to drown?!" "Master, carest thou not that we perish?" (4:38). In their fear Christ's posse takes a little more attitude with Him than they probably should.

When the disciples come bursting in, Jesus does something extremely cool. Picture it: Jesus is chillin' in His cabin when the disciples disturb His rest. Instead of rising in glory and conjuring up some spectacular display of His power, He simply stands up, rebukes the wind and tells the waves to shut up.

We often get so distracted by our storms that we forget Jesus' presence and power.

Mark quotes Jesus as saying to the sea: "Peace, be still" (4:39)—basically He's saying "shut up and stay that way." It's like Jesus is driving around with the wind and water in the backseat of His car, and He turns around and says, "Stop it, and don't start up again on this trip"—and the elements obey. Jesus proves His awesome control to the disciples without breaking a sweat.

Jesus had His disciples' backs, but they were still frightened by their violent physical surroundings. We too often get so distracted by our storms that we forget Jesus' presence and power. We get so caught up in our own struggles that we fail to see them from God's perspective.

Do you ever doubt the Lord's promises even though deep down you know that He has it under control? Jesus had a message for His disciples who became frightened and gave Him attitude: "Why are ye fearful, O ye of little faith?" (8:26). In more common vernacular He's saying, "Don't be scared. I got you." Wanda from the popular TV series *In Living Color* was not the first to say, "I got you"; long before sitcoms came along, Jesus proved that He could be trusted.

Unfortunately it's easy for us to get caught up in the wind and waves. We often fail to praise God until the storm is over and we can clearly see the reality of our situation.

Look at the disciples. Only after Jesus calmed their tempest did they marvel at His power, saying: "What manner of man is this, that even the winds and the sea obey Him!" In their trial, they felt alone, but, fortunately, the purpose and value of the storm was not entirely lost on them. Through their struggle, Christ's power was revealed to them.

> *We often fail to praise God until the storm is over.*

You Have Something to Learn from Your Storm

There are lessons to be learned from every storm. Storms come mostly to teach us about the Lord, because not everything about God can be learned in Sunday school. Even if you know your theology, you can only understand some aspects of God when He reveals them to you in your life.

The disciples asked: "What manner of man is this?" (Matt. 8:27). "Who is this Jesus who has taken us from the frightening brink of death to complete peace?" We too should use our storms to question and learn more about the person of Christ.

Let me rewind. When Jesus tells the disciples to follow Him into the boat, it's still early in their careers. The storm that comes is part of a necessary process for increasing their faith. Jesus is saying, "You have to understand that we're still in light water here. We haven't gotten to where I am going to pick fights in synagogues. We haven't gotten to Bethany where they are going to throw stones at Me. We haven't gotten to where they are going to try to *kill* Me. If you are going to be able to handle all of that, you first have to go through some

> *No matter where you are in your relationship with God, life storms will come.*

stuff to prepare you for the reality of what's to come." So there was a serious tempest, meant to teach them in new ways.

Let's take a moment to extrapolate some of the lessons the disciples' story teaches. First, it suggests that, no matter where you are in your relationship with God, life storms will come. In fact, the higher you go with God, the stronger the storms will become. When you're first starting out on your faith walk, you will have small storms, and when God calls you to larger assignments, you will have larger storms.

Sometimes we ask, "Why do storms have to happen in the first place?" Well, there are different types of storms, and they serve different purposes.

Some storms, like Jonah's, are correcting storms. Maybe you've been going the wrong way, and God says, "I need to blow you back onto the road where I want you, because I have a plan for your life. I know what it is that I have for you to accomplish, and you've been headed in your own direction for far too long." We need these types of storms to get us back on the right course.

Some storms, however, are demonic, distracting storms. For example, look at when Jesus was standing out on the stormy sea and Peter stepped out of the boat and started walking across the water to Him. As long as Peter kept his eyes on Jesus, he stayed above the surface, but as soon as he looked at the tempest raging around him, he began to sink. Sometimes storms come just to distract you. Don't pay attention to them. Keep your eyes on Jesus.

Refining storms fall into a third category. They come into your life when God is preparing you for a new season. God has work to do in you and things to teach you. Sometimes you have rough edges that need smoothing over, and you're not going to learn through sunshine and Sunday school but only through trials and tribulations.

There was a great response to the disciples' great storm.

Sometimes we can't even categorize our storms, because they're too large for us to comprehend. The storm the disciples faced was no ordinary little shower. Since they were fishermen, they would have known how to classify weather, and they called this one a whopper, a "*great* tempest."

You've probably dealt with multiple common storms, but every once in a while a great whale of a tempest hits you, and it hurts you in a way you've never been hurt before. It messes with stuff that has been left alone in the past. It pokes you in places you didn't even know were sore. Through the pain it challenges you while bringing you to revelation and understanding.

Your storm is getting you ready for the new level or dimension God has planned for you. Ride out your storm while it lasts. When God finishes teaching you, you'll be ready for the next step!

Don't Stay Silent in Your Storm!

There was a great response to the disciples' great storm. They didn't just sit around quietly on the deck as their boat was buffeted by gales and torrents of water; instead, they turned to Jesus. Like them, in order to grow through your storms, you have to go to God in prayer.

Maybe you don't see the disciples' prayer in the text, but it's there. Sometimes we think of prayer as being nice and cute. We think of it as being: "Now I lay me down to sleep. I pray the Lord my soul to keep. If I should die before I wake, I pray the Lord my soul to take. If I should live for many days, I pray the Lord will guide my ways. Ahhhh, yes. Ooooooh, God, You are *awesome*."

You have to get real with God, and you have a God who can get real with you.

Now, don't get me wrong. There is a time for such prayers; this just isn't always the way we feel like praying when we're in the thick of it.

In the text, when the disciples are in the midst of their storm, they pray a very serious prayer: "Lord, save us!" They are being honest with God, and their questions of "Jesus, don't You care what's happening? *What is going on here?*" are genuine. When they ask, "Jesus, do You even see what's going on with us?" that's prayer too.

Sometimes you have to get real with God, and you have a God who can get real with you. You have a Savior who can talk. He doesn't speak King James—He speaks to who you are, where you are. Don't be afraid to be honest: "God, what's up with this situation? Help me! God, help me!"

You might get religious at church, but don't get religious with God. He can see straight through your pretentions, so pray in earnest. Grandma used to call this kind of prayer "having a little talk with Jesus." Tell God what you're going through. Tell Him how you feel. Tell Him what's on your mind. Then, sit there and wait until He talks back to you.

Do you know that if you wait long enough, God will respond? God's will will be done in God's time. God will fix your situation when it needs to be fixed.

That said, God doesn't always operate on our time. While the disciples are freaking out about the situation above deck, Jesus is asleep. The Bible isn't specific as to how long He sleeps, but it is clear that He lets the storm rage for a while. Finally, He wakes up, tells the storm to shut up and rebukes the disciples' weak faith. There is a time limit to the storm in the text, and I hope that is encouraging to you.

Meanwhile, as you're being tossed about by the tempest, take some time to learn about yourself. Ask: "God, before this storm, where was I? What was I doing? Where was I wrong, and how was I disobedient? Did I have as much faith as I thought? How do I doubt You? Are You showing me things I need to see before I can reach the next dimension? What do I need to learn?"

Sometimes God places a mirror in front of you in the form of a storm. As human beings, we're quick to point out what others need to learn or need to change, but we often turn a blind eye to how God desires to transform our own lives. Get real with yourself.

In addition to teaching you about yourself, storms teach you how to deal with situations and relationships. What were you paying attention to before your storm? Who were you connected to? Why was Jesus so absent from your life that you had to go looking for Him when the storm struck?

Through your storms, God will reveal the relationships that you need to strengthen and those you need to cut. He will refine what is *good* into that which is *best* for your life.

God is Greater Than Your Storm

Surviving your storm begins with having Jesus on your boat. You should contemplate: "What manner of man is this?" When the seas of life get rough, the first person you should turn to is Christ. He has something to teach you through your storms. There is always something new to learn about His purposes and His promises.

You might feel as if you can't see clearly because your storm is blotting out all the light in your life, but I'm here to tell you that it is going to be all right. If you feel ready to give up, I'm here to tell you that the final bell has not rung. You haven't even reached the twelfth round.

> *Surviving your storm begins with having Jesus on your boat.*

Don't take your mouthpiece out. Don't throw in the towel. Keep on fighting, keep on believing and keep on keeping on. God won't let you fight alone.

Grandma used to say that the Lord makes ways out of no ways. I used to listen to her and think, "Okay, but what you really mean is that there was just a way that I didn't see." In reality *there wasn't a way*. Do you believe that God will make a way out of no way?

When I think of "making a way," I remember an old football illustration. I used to say that I was like a halfback, and God was like a fullback. God would plow through the defensive line and open up a hole so that I could run the play. Storms have helped me understand, however, that I'm neither the fullback nor the halfback.

When the winds and waves hit you so hard that you couldn't run even if the hole were there, God will be the fullback, and God will be the halfback. God will carry the ball in one hand and you in the other, break through the opposition, carry you to the end zone and put you down so you can look back at everyone and declare, "Touchdown!"

Even if you don't think you can make it past all of the big, scary things lined up in front of you that are set on flattening you into the ground, God will make a way. No storm is bigger than God.

The great thing about God is that while He is strong and able to help us fight our battles, He is also our Comforter—a heart-fixer and mind-regulator. If you feel like crying, go ahead and cry on His lap. If you are upset, be upset in His presence, because He is able to take care of you.

Then again, although God is greater than your storm, He doesn't promise it won't keep raging. He doesn't promise to make the journey easy. It might not even seem like He's around. From time to time, your little squall might feel like a hurricane, and you might feel like you're facing it alone.

Consider for a moment the struggles of Dr. Martin Luther King. We celebrate Dr. King for what he preached, but we also celebrate the fact that he preached it in the midst of his own personal journey. While he was working to bring a voice to others, he had to keep fighting for his own. He wasn't criticized solely by those on the other side of the political spectrum; some of his own folk didn't believe in his cause.

Notably, Dr. King's famous "Letter from Birmingham City Jail," written after he had been jailed for a peaceful protest against segregation, was written not to atheists but to preachers. Even the godly men he might have expected to come alongside him in his struggle voiced instead their opposition to his methods.

Take a lesson from Dr. King: even if you find that your naysayers outnumber your supporters, keep going. Focusing on the storms and

Sometimes you have to keep on praying, keep on fasting, keep on praising; just stay where you are.

forgetting your ultimate destiny will distract you from living out your greater purpose.

I need you to know that your storm won't be over until you learn your lesson. If you keep fighting God and never turn to Him to find out why you're facing the storm in the first place, you'll never get out of it. But, if you maintain a teachable spirit and learn what God wants you to know, He'll bring you into the calm.

Finding Calm after Your Storm

You probably know the Scripture: "Weeping may endure for a night, but joy cometh in the morning" (Ps. 30:5). Have you ever noticed, though, that sometimes "the morning" is not tomorrow morning or even the morning after that? Sometimes you have to keep on praying, keep on fasting, keep on praising; just stay where you are. Even if it isn't this morning, you are one morning closer to when whatever you're going through will be over, because you know that *this too shall pass.*

Matthew says that after the storm, there was a great

calm. You can't rush past that. When the text says that there was a "great tempest," it means that it was bigger than normal storms, so when it says that there was a "great calm," it means that the calm is better than the "calm" the disciples thought they had before the storm.

When God takes you to a storm, He takes you through a storm.

When your storm gets finished with you, you will be better off than you were before trouble hit. In other words, you may think that the storm came and messed up what you had, but apparently what you had wasn't what was supposed to be. God has something better for you on the other side.

I'm not going to lie to you; it might get hard. The important thing is to keep your eyes on Jesus. You might be crying, but you are hoping; you are crying, but you're believing. Some people might not understand your struggle, but keep going, knowing that when your storm is over, your life is going to be better than what you thought was good.

Even if you're in a time of going through and aren't enjoying it, start praising God right now that when you come out of it, you are going to exit into a great calm.

Can you trust that there is a blessing waiting for you on the opposite shore? New life and a new kind of peace come in the calm after the storm.

When you finally reach the calm, you may notice that you have lost some things along the way. Not everybody who was with you before the storm is going to be with you on the other side. You may lose some people and you may lose some stuff in the wind and waves of your struggle, but, like David, you can claim: "The Lord is my Shepherd; I shall not want" (Ps. 23:1).

I know it's difficult, but storms test your real relationships. If you can't handle a storm together, then you weren't really together in the calm. I don't know about you, but I need some folk who can handle some wind. I need some folk who can handle some waves.

Think about the best day in your past. Your tomorrows are going to be so much better than that day because when God takes you *to* a storm, He takes you *through* a storm.

When God brings you through the storm, as He will in His own time, don't pretend like you did it all on your own. Take your fake halo off and say, "If it hadn't been for the Lord on my side, I wouldn't be here now. I didn't have a way out. My mind couldn't figure it out. My heart couldn't take it anymore. But Jesus made a way out of no way." Amen.

Once you've reached the other side, be an encouragement to those around you who are still feeling the mighty winds and seeing the tall waves. They need to know that it's going to be all right. Tell them, as I'm telling you now, "You're going to make it. You will survive. It will change. It's going to be all right." Thank God for this truth.

Do you remember how I said that your life is going to be a great story? God wants to grow you through your storms, so don't worry if life doesn't always feel like it's going to turn out happily ever after.

Now, I don't know the timing of your storm, and God has not given me a prophetic word to announce to you that it is going to end right now, but He has given me a word to tell you that your storm has an appointed time, and it will end.

I'm not saying it's going to be all right today, tonight or tomorrow. But I *am* saying that soon and very soon, the Lord is going to make a way. The Lord is going to lead you into the calm after your storm, completing another chapter of the exciting, rich story of your life. Praise God!

Discussion Questions:

1. Read Matthew 8:18–22, 28–34, the text surrounding the disciples' experience with the storm. Pay special attention to the dialogue. Why does Jesus respond the way He does to the disciples' concerns?

2. Are you headed into a storm, in the thick of a storm or coming out of a storm? Are you focusing on the "winds and waves" of your circumstance, or are you focused on Christ? How might reevaluating your focus change your situation?

3. What might it look like for you to "get real" with God in order to experience His cleansing power? Check out First John 1:9. Why do we hesitate to confess our struggles and fears if God already knows everything about them?

4. Sometimes we're concerned our storms may damage our relationships or our social standing, but verses like Luke 3:10–14 and Matthew 19:16–21 teach us not to focus on earthly advancement. We need to hold our worldly possessions with an open hand and freely give of ourselves to others—no matter what the risk. What are you most afraid of losing? How can you turn your material goods and relationships over to God's control so He can be free to move in your life?

Action Point: God can make a way out of no way. Think back to moments in your past when Christ has come through for you despite seemingly insurmountable storms. Praise Him for those times and dedicate yourself to continually, fully trusting Him for your future.

2

CLEANING UP YOUR ACT

Fearfulness and trembling are come upon me, and horror hath overwhelmed me.
And I said, Oh that I had wings like a dove! for then would I fly away, and be at rest. Psalm 55:5–6

I have a confession to make: I'm somewhat of a cluttery half-slob. Now, that's not to say that I'm a dirty person. In fact, I take a shower every day—even twice a day in the summer! My organizational skills, however, could use some help.

My military background has given me an appreciation for order, so I always *start* with things nice and clean, but I find it hard to *keep* everything organized. Do you know what I'm talking about? I pull out a book and leave it on a chair. I read some mail and put it on the desk. I drive my car around and throw some trash on the floor. Before you know it, stuff's piling up everywhere.

By the time I decide to do something about the mess, it looks like too much to handle. My desk, my car and my space in my house—as designated by my wife, Sister Waller—suddenly look too, well, *cluttery*.

Because I travel so much, I've taken on what Cornell West calls a hotel personality. It's wonderful to stay in hotels.

You can throw stuff all over the place and head out for the day, yet when you get back to the room, the bed will be made, your books will be arranged and fresh towels will be neatly hung on the rack. If it's a really nice hotel, there might even be a note on your pillow from the cleaning lady saying she hopes you enjoy your stay.

When I return home, it takes me a second to realize I'm no longer in a five-star hotel—nobody's going to clean up my messes for me. No cleaning fairy is going to come and wave her wand and make it all go away. I take one look at my office, see everything I've left lying about and decide I don't want to work there. I'm embarrassed to be seen in my trash-filled car, so I ask Sister Waller if I can drive hers. When visitors come over, I act all phony—asking them to excuse my desk as if it just got messy and wasn't already that way when they called to see if I was available.

Finally, when I realize I absolutely *have* to do something about all my stuff, I start sifting through it. And you know what? When the garbage bags come out and I take time to sit down and go through everything, I can handle what I thought was too much.

Now, you're probably sitting there thinking, *WHAT does this man keep on his desk and in his car, and why is he going on and on about it?* It isn't about the desk. Stay with me.

Facing Your Stuff

How about you? Do you know what it's like to make a clean start in life—only to discover you're soon back at your old ways, piling stuff in every nook and cranny? Have you ever examined your life and discovered your mess was too big to deal with? It's tempting to merely ignore your problems in those situations. It's easy to go into denial to avoid your mess. At some point, however, you have to face reality.

In Psalm 55 we find David trying to wish himself into a different reality. When he says, "Oh that I had wings like a dove!" what he's really saying is, "I wish I had dove's wings!" Now, humans are never going to fly around on wings, so someone should have explained to David that wishing wasn't going to get him anywhere. No, it wasn't easy to be the king of Israel in turbulent times, but David should have just bucked up and dealt with it. Instead, he tried to wish his mess away.

Don't do what David did. Instead, say like Dorothy in *The Wizard of Oz*, "We're not in Kansas anymore." Learn to assess and deal with the reality of your circumstances instead of holding onto the past or some self-created version of the present. If you try to live in your own fantasy,

> *Even if you feel like you're in over your head, God still has your situation under control.*

the real world will become less and less desirable to you.

You may wish you hadn't made that mistake, but you did. You may wish you hadn't said that thing, but you did. You may wish you had another job, but you don't. You may wish you had more money, but you don't. Listen: You live where you live. You work where you work. Your mess is your mess.

If you find yourself feeling like you can't handle your situation and wishing things were different, check out Psalm 55's positive message. Look at David: even though he wishes life were different, he holds on.

Do you see the invisible shout out from God to you

in the text? You have hope, because you aren't lost in your mess. Even if you feel like you're in over your head, God still has your situation under control. Even if your situation feels wrong, you still got up this morning. You're still alive. You're still in your right mind. You have another opportunity to handle whatever is bothering you.

Take that opportunity. Once you've assessed the reality of your situation, you need to accept that you are where you are, and *there* is where the Lord is going to work.

David fails to accept his situation and his location. In his wishing he says he wants to go somewhere else to get some rest. He exclaims, "I want some wings to fly away!"

Now, whenever I'm looking at a text, I run several analyses. I start with grammatical exegesis: "How does the language reveal the meaning of what is written?" Then, I move to social exegesis: "How should the historical, cultural perspective of the time impact my reading?" Finally, I do some geographical exegesis, and this is where I got stuck in Psalm 55. Why? Well, I'm telling you, I checked every continent, every country and every city on every map I could find, and I couldn't locate anywhere named "Away."

I understand that at the time, David just wanted out of his situation, but I say, "Hold up, King David—you have drama in your life because you're the king of Israel. I hate to break it to you, but no matter where you go, you're still going to be the king of Israel. This place of Away doesn't exist, so you aren't going to fix anything by changing your address. Fly anywhere you please, you're still going to be King David—and because you're King David, someone isn't going to like you. Sorry Davey, but you have to suck it up. You are where you are."

All right, so David had it *up to here* with everything going on in his life, and fearfulness and trembling had come upon him and overwhelmed him. He wanted to get out of his messy joint: "If I only had wings of a dove, I could fly away and be at rest." Now, many of us have sung songs containing this phrase about doves' wings thinking that what David is talking about is a good thing. What he's really saying, though, is that he wants to run away from the issues he needs to face. Bad idea, David.

Doves aren't built to handle hard weather.

Escape doesn't come when you remove yourself from places but when you claim freedom for your own mind. At some point, you have to decide that you don't need to run away from everything in order to get your rest—you need to get your rest right where you are.

Weak Wings Won't Work

When David says, "Oh that I had wings like a dove!" (55:6), he isn't only spending time ineffectively wishing for what isn't—he's also putting his faith in something that can't help him instead of trusting the Lord to provide. How so? Well, let's talk about birds.

Doves are the weakest-winged bird of the species. Do you know what doves do when it starts raining? They find a tree to perch in and wait out the storm. Doves aren't built to handle hard weather. I mean, come on, David! Pick a hawk or something—not a dove! Everybody knows they're pretty pathetically fragile little things; the pop artist Prince even wrote a song about how doves cry.

Still, if we're honest, there are a whole bunch of us who

try to escape on weak wings when pressure comes. What are weak wings? Trying to drink yourself away, trying to smoke yourself away and trying to drug yourself away are all examples of poorly equipping yourself to face the real storms of your life. If you're trying to avoid dealing with your situation, you have weak wings.

Pay attention now, because sex, drugs and rock'n'roll aren't the only things people use to escape; holier-than-thou mentalities and fake religiosity are also signs of spiritual weakness. You've heard of the German philosopher/ sociologist/communist Karl Marx, right? While I don't agree with everything Marx says, I can ride with him when he says that the superfluous emotionalism of the church has become an opiate for the people. Stay with me for a minute.

> *You need to stop going to church to get an emotional fix and start going to be empowered with the Word.*

Here's where the message hits home. Yes, it's a weak wing to drink yourself away. *Preach it, brother.* Yes, it's a weak wing to smoke yourself away. *Amen.* Yes, it's a weak wing to try to buy yourself away from your problems. *Mmhmm.* But it's also a weak wing to praise yourself away if you are not being intentional about really getting into the Word and revolutionizing your situation according to God's will. *Halle—. Wait . . . what?*

No, I didn't just go crazy, and yes, I do love emotionalism in the church. I love having a knockdown, drag-out worship experience, waving my hands and praising. That said, I preach at the Enon Tabernacle Baptist Church—not at Club Enon, and going to church should not look like going clubbing. Worshiping Christ does not involve bellying up to the pew to take a couple shots of emotionalism and chase them with music.

You need to stop going to church to get an emotional fix and start going to be empowered with the Word. Going to church with no interest in dealing with your real sins looks like this: You walk into church. The preacher preaches. You say to the preacher, "Ah, your message really hit me today. You got up close and personal with that sermon— you were on my toes!" Then you go back to the same hell you had been living in. The

You want wings like eagles. Why? Because not only can they fly through storms— they can fly above storms.

next week, you're back: "Oh, Reverend, that message really hit home. You were really on my toes!" Then you return to living the same away. When are you going to move your feet? When you leave, you should be saying that although you may have been down, you are not going to stay down, because you are going forth in the name of Jesus!

Weak wings aren't going to get you anywhere. If you want some *real* wings, look to Isaiah: "They that wait upon the LORD shall renew their strength; they shall mount up with wings as eagles; they shall run, and not be weary; and they shall walk, and not faint" (40:31).

You want wings like eagles. Why? Because not only can they fly *through* storms—they can fly *above* storms. If you're going to pray for wings, pray for the ones that make you strong and help you renew your faith and trust in the Lord—not weak wings that get you into the middle of a storm you can't handle.

Now, David handles it all the wrong way, but I know
where he's coming from. I get what he's going through. I too
have faced times when I can't wait to get as far as possible
from where I live. Sometimes, when I'm traveling and the
plane lifts out of Philadelphia, I feel like I can breathe again.
It's like a deep, freeing exhale. Then, when I return and my
plane is taxiing down the runway, I can almost feel pressure
building on my chest. At those times I'm saying, "Oh, Lord,
here I go back into all my stress—back into the land of too
many demands and too much anxiety." But Philadelphia is
not my problem—I don't need to fly away on weak wings.
There I am, giving all my power to Philly, and the city is not
the real issue—I am my own problem.

What If I'm My Own Problem?

You see, some of the drama in your life isn't just about
where you are, it's about *who* you are. When you're in the
middle of a situation, you need not only to accept your
circumstances and location—you should also strive to ob-
jectively understand your role in the problem. If you find
yourself repeatedly ending up in the same, complicated situations, you need to analyze whether or not you are the cause
and not the victim.

Don't blame others or geographical locations when your
life is disconnected from God. Face your issues and physical
situation, and start dealing with the internal issues that got
you into your mess in the first place.

Ask yourself: "What am I allowing to distract me from
my purpose?" Have you given your purpose to a place or
your job or to someone who used to be in your life? It's time
to reclaim who you truly are in light of God's promises.

When you give things other than Christ your power, you allow them to control you. It's like you're calling them up every morning to ask: "Can I get up today? Am I allowed to smile today? Is it all right if I have fun today? Do you mind if I walk around like the child of God that I am today?"

Let me unpack this in reverse order. In NA (Narcotics Anonymous) and AA (Alcoholics Anonymous), they teach that in order for you to escape addiction, you have to change the people, places and things in your life. Now, I'm not saying this can't be a true step toward healing, but you aren't fully healed until you've reached the point where people, places and things don't really matter. The truth is, whether or not you're in a certain environment, you have to maintain control over yourself.

Am I talking to you? Are you listening? I want to be careful about what I'm saying here because I understand that you may be struggling with something like a domestic violence situation, and yes, you should get out of it. No woman should ever let a man lay an unwanted hand on her. That said, once you've gotten out geographically, you can't assume the work is over. The problem might not be your fault, but you do have to examine what drew you into the relationship in the first place. You need to make sure that who you are isn't going to get you back into another similar, dangerous situation.

If you're committed to dealing with your internal issues, you can claim God's power in your life. If you turn your sins over to Jesus, He'll help you through.

The Bible says that the Lord will prepare a table for you in the midst of your enemies. That means if you trust God, you have the power to remain in the middle of your problems and to calmly ask your enemies to please pass the potatoes. Don't wait until everything around you fixes it-self—strive to make who you are match up to who God has called you to be now.

Are you willing to allow God to transform your situation, your life and even you?

As long as you have the right Christ-perspective, your situation doesn't really matter. You can be in a recession, or you can have money. You can be eating steak, or you can be eating oodles of noodles. You know it's going to be all right, because as long as God is for you, no one can be against you. Are you willing to allow Him to transform your situation, your life and even *you*?

Time to Clean Up!

Now, I've been taking a negative position and talking about what David was missing in the text, but, to be fair, he comes to the right conclusion in the end. David has a way of complaining and feeling bad at the beginning of many of the psalms, but he always closes out with a conviction to praise the Lord and to trust Him. We should have that same fervor.

Say, "I'm going to stand right here, where I am, and fight this battle, and I'm going to trust God to have my back. I'm not going to wish my life away. I'm not going to try to escape from my problems on weak wings."

I know it can be frightening when you feel like you're standing by yourself. When you stand, however, God will send His angels to care for you. Even if you feel like your back is up against the wall and there's no way out, God is there, and He has the power to lift you out of the situation. When you trust and stand on God's promises, God will stand in for you. I'm not telling you that trusting Christ is the *easiest* way, but it is the *best* way.

You could take the quick way out—abdicate your anointing, your call and your responsibility. But listen: you don't want to lose your place in God's kingdom trying to please man. Life might seem easier on the outside, but things won't be right on the inside. I don't know about you, but I'd much rather have a problem with mankind and be right with God than the other way around because I know that, unlike people, my God will be unfailingly faithful if I strive to follow His will.

Do you need to make some phone calls, patch up some relations, drop some things that shouldn't have power over your life, and take your joy and peace back? Do it. No person has power over you unless you give it to them. Decide for yourself that *this* is the day that the Lord

> *You don't want to lose your place in God's kingdom trying to please man.*

has made and that you will "rejoice and be glad in it" (Ps. 118:24).

God's praise should continually be in our mouths, because He is our aid in sticking out the bad times, wading through all the stuff we've accumulated and emerging clean and with wings like eagles.

You might have to deal with some stuff in your life, but remember: you can't run away because there's no place called "Away." Nobody is going to clean up your messes for you, and no one—do you hear me?—*no one* can fix your life, *except* Jesus.

If you're experiencing the challenges that come from trying to live your life without God, stop flying around on weak wings. Give your life to Christ, and you'll feel real, unspeakable joy and peace that passes all understanding. Give your life to Christ, and He'll meet you where you are.

Once you accept the reality of your situation, Jesus will help you clean up your stuff. Time to start sorting.

Discussion Questions:

1. Is your life cluttered? What can you do to start cleaning up your mess? What people can you call to come alongside you and hold you accountable to moving forward in Christ?

2. Are you "flying around on weak wings"? What concrete steps can you take to be transformed from a weak dove into a strong, godly eagle?

3. Hebrews 10:25 encourages us to "not forsake the assembling of ourselves together." Why do you go to church? Are you willing to be spiritually challenged by the Word and fellow believers?

4. Each of us has a specific purpose in Christ. Read Romans 12:4–8. Which gifts has God given you? How are you using them? Are you allowing anything to distract you from your purpose?

Action Point: Take a moment to analyze your life and the things that define you. (Thinking about how you spend the majority of your time and money is a good way to do this.) Now think about how you'd like to be defined and what you'd like your life to reflect. Pray, asking the Lord to help you focus on Him and His plans for you above all else.

3

BELIEVING GOD

But after long abstinence Paul stood forth in the midst of them, and said, Sirs, ye should have hearkened unto me, and not have loosed from Crete, and to have gained this harm and loss. And now I exhort you to be of good cheer: for there shall be no loss of any man's life among you, but of the ship. For there stood by me this night the angel of God, whose I am, and whom I serve, saying, Fear not, Paul; thou must be brought before Caesar: and, lo, God hath given thee all them that sail with thee. Wherefore, sirs, be of good cheer: for I believe God, that it shall be even as it was told me. Acts 27:21–25

D o you believe God? Lots of people believe that God exists—they believe *in* God. That's different, however, from believing God to do what He's promised.

Maybe you're finding yourself unable to balance what God has said He'll do in your life with what's currently going on, but trusting God means following Him—no matter what your environment looks like. Believing God means maintaining a theology of hope and determination that says, "I shall not be moved, because my Father is greater than anything this world can throw at me."

I think the African-American church offers a unique perspective on unconditional hope. Unfortunately, when people talk about the distinctiveness of African-American Christianity, they often get caught up in the light and trite aspects of black folks' religious experiences. Just about every time the black church is depicted in movies or on television, there's a silly preacher, a lot of pulpit gymnastics and several way-out older women shouting and feeling the Spirit. Now, don't get me wrong: I love good preaching, and I love good singing, and I'm glad to have a place where we can let God have His way. I'm just saying that our roots run much deeper than some Holy Ghost happy hour.

If you want to get into our distinctive theology, look at what Cornell West has to say about radical Christianity and subversive joy in his book *Prophetic Fragments*. He says that there is an unusual theology of hope in the church in general and that, especially in the African-American church, there is an ability to hope against hope. Our determined faith says that *we shall not be moved*. We keep smiles on our faces—no matter how much we're struggling—because we know that God will help us make it through.

Look at our history. Our ancestors sat in slavery and sang songs of hope. They faced dark times and had difficult struggles, but they kept praising God. They dealt with the reality of the Jim Crow laws and faced people like Bull Connor—yet they maintained their ability to see beauty in the world. They kept playing music and dancing. They affirmed that God existed, and they trusted Him.

As slaves, my grandfather and great grandfather had every reason to want to give up and throw in the towel, yet they kept going—trusting that a day of freedom would come. You know why? Because they had a theology that said that no matter how bad the storm, no matter how difficult the situation, the key is to keep believing God.

My grandparents didn't sit around waiting until heaven to catch a glimpse of God; instead, they believed the Lord was working out His kingdom in their midst. Grandma used to say, "It's not just about pie in the sky by and by; it's also about ham and yams where I am." In other words, "I am going to keep praising God—for the hope He has given me for the future but also for the reality I'm living in today."

> *I am going to keep praising God.*

Acts 27:21–25 gives us two different perspectives on trusting God. Paul trusts God and follows Him from the beginning, so he's able to say "I believe God"; whereas the sailors—who try to handle the situation on their own—face some disconcerting struggles.

Let me give you some background: The story starts with Paul and these sailors on a prison ship near Crete. Paul, who had gotten himself into trouble with his preaching, was being taken to Rome as a prisoner to give an account of himself before Caesar.

When the men set sail, they're aware that the weather conditions are less than ideal. Paul is convicted against leaving—foreseeing loss and potential death at sea—so he counsels the sailors to remain at port for the winter. The other men, however, decide they know better. They think they know *exactly what they're doing* and just how to handle the situation, so they ignore Paul's misgivings.

While Paul recognized the purpose God had for him and trusted Him to see him through, the other sailors refused to listen to spiritual wisdom, recklessly insisting on leading their lives their own way. As we'll see, these two distinct ways of responding to God have different outcomes.

Which way will *you* choose to respond? My hope is that you'll be able to say, "I believe God will see me through and will fulfill the purpose He has for my life."

God's Mercy is Greater Than Your Mistakes

It's good to strive to perfectly follow God's will, but the truth is that sometimes you're going to mess up. You're going to make mistakes. Look at the sailors—even though Paul counseled them against heading out to sea, they didn't listen and their dismissive attitudes got all the men into trouble.

Trusting the Lord doesn't guarantee you won't get into some rough waters.

Ignoring the light wind at port, the sailors soon found themselves confronted with a big, bad storm. The King James calls the storm "Euroclydon" from the Greek word *eurakulon*, meaning a nor'easter. This monster storm was no light drizzle.

Check out Paul's admonition at the beginning of the verse we're examining: "Sirs, ye should have hearkened unto me, and not have loosed from Crete, and to have gained this harm and loss" (Acts 27:21). Even though the sailors were the ones who made the mistake, Paul was threatened by the wind and waves too. You see, trusting the Lord doesn't guarantee you won't get into some rough waters.

But guess what? Even in the chaos, Paul's message is hopeful. In verse 22 he continues, "And now I exhort you to be of good cheer: for there shall be no loss of any man's life among you." Picture it: the storm is raging. The sailors are trying to handle the situation on their own, but it isn't working. It looks like they're going to die, yet Paul gives them a message—delivered to him by an angel—that says everything's going to work out.

The sailors never should have left Crete, yet God had compassion on them. He sent an angel to deliver a comforting message in the midst of their storm. His mercy was bigger than their mess. He saved them when they should have sunk.

God will work around your failures, because He knows your potential.

The sailors may have deserved death, but they received protection. Like them, we also receive blessings above and beyond what we merit. If we were treated with real justice, we'd never win the love of the Lord. Why? Because we're all sinners, and the Bible says "the wages of sin is death" (Rom. 6:23). We can't do anything to be worthy of God's grace, yet He gives it freely. God loves us so much that He's willing to forgive us and restore us to our purpose in Him—even when we *really* screw up. Praise God that He looks beyond our mistakes to give us first, second and even third chances!

God knows that you're a fallible human. He knew you before He formed you in your mother's belly. He knows your gifts and your flaws. He knows what you're capable of, and He has a plan for you. He'll work around your failures, because He knows your potential.

The Lord's blessings are abundant and unmerited. You might ask, "How can that be? Why would God bless me even though I don't deserve it?"

Let me give an example. As the pastor of the Enon

Tabernacle Baptist Church, I find myself doing a considerable amount of traveling. A couple of times I've shown up at the airport with a coach ticket only to run into a member of my congregation who works at an airline. I'll hear, "Oh! Bless you, Pastor Waller," see a shuffle behind the counter and suddenly find myself upgraded to first class. Now, I only paid for coach. I only *deserved* coach. But I was blessed beyond what I merited.

I'm not trying to tell you that God is just around to give you stuff and upgrade you to first class. What I am saying is: Because God loves us, He takes care of us in a way that goes above and beyond anything we could earn.

> *God's going to allow storms to break up anything in your life that is making you arrogant and disobedient.*

You may be upset with me—thinking I'm saying we can live any old way we want without negative effects because God will always forgive us—but that's not the point I'm trying to make. What I'm saying is that even though God can work around our mistakes, our actions have very real consequences.

Disobedience Leads to Difficulties

Watch what happens in the text. The angel tells Paul and the sailors, "You're not going to die." Great! But then he continues, "But that boat you had? Yeah, you're gonna lose that." By refusing to listen to Paul's admonishment, the sailors failed to believe God, and it landed them in trouble.

Because the sailors thought their profession meant they knew more about weather and safety than some religious guy, they lost the physical representation of their livelihood and their arrogance: their boat. Because their boat was not necessary to do God's will, it was taken away from them.

Are you paying attention? Sometimes you need storms to break up the vehicles of your disobedience so you can go before God. Because God wants you to walk closely with Him, He's going to allow storms to break up anything in your life that is making you arrogant and disobedient.

The truth of the matter is that storms are not really bad; they're the answer to the poor conditions that precede them. Right before storms, the barometric pressure is high and there is a confluence of cold and hot air. Where I live in eastern Pennsylvania, pre-storm weather is claustrophobic—it gets muggy and sticky and all-around miserable. Then, after the rain, the humidity is cleared away, the skies are blue, and you can breathe again.

You see, sometimes you need God to send a storm into your life, because you're not going to get out of whatever sticky mess you're in without one. You aren't going to leave your problem alone until a storm comes along to break it up. God says, "I'm not going to let you keep living in your foolishness. I'm not going to let you die in sin. If I have to break up your boat, I'm going to, because I have a plan for your life."

Ask around: lots of Christians can tell you that, yes, bad things have happened to them—but God has led them and taught them through those storms. Storms are often necessary to clear away the icky stuff in our life to help us set a straighter course.

If you read past our verses for this chapter into Acts 28, you'll find God using the shipwreck to allow Paul to minister to an island tribe. God deals with the sailors' arrogance and then uses the situation for greater good. In a similar fashion the Lord will use your storms to strengthen you—it just might mean losing some things along the way.

God Fulfills His Purposes

Through the calm and through the storm, God had His hand on Paul's life. Since Paul believed in and trusted God, God wasn't about to allow the sailors' disobedience to mess with Paul's purpose.

God's plan is partly explained in the message of the angel God sent to comfort Paul: "Fear not, Paul; thou must be brought before Caesar: and, lo, God hath given thee all them that sail with thee" (Acts 27:24). The angel told Paul everything would work out—not because Paul was special but because God had given him a necessary purpose. God wanted him to go before Caesar, so Paul went before Caesar.

God had had a plan for Paul since before he was born.

The really cool thing about Paul's story is that it fits into a much larger narrative. You see, God had had a plan for Paul since before he was born. Let's rewind back to the Old Testament for a moment to see how Paul going before Caesar connected to God's purpose of spreading the gospel message.

Open your Bible and flip to the book of Daniel with me. In chapter 2 we find Daniel interpreting a dream for King Nebuchadnezzar. In one of Daniel's prophetic analyses, he talks about a rock that crashes into a statue and then grows to be a mountain that fills the whole earth (Dan. 2:31–45). This prophecy is fulfilled in the New Testament, starting with Christ. No, Jesus wasn't made out of stone—but He did crash into the kingdom of Rome in the sense that His teachings undermined Roman culture.

After Christ's death and resurrection, His disciples continued to advocate for His truth. Here's where Paul comes in. God needed Paul to stand before Caesar to show that the "Jesus movement" didn't end with Christ's crucifixion. Paul was part of the "mountain" in that, by preaching the gospel, Paul helped Christianity spread.

When you strive to be within God's will, He'll keep you on track.

Did you catch that? Paul wasn't just some guy God randomly selected on the spur of the moment. Things that happened hundreds upon hundreds of years earlier led to Paul standing trial before Caesar. When God sent the angel to tell Paul it was going to be all right, it's like He was saying, "Listen, Paul, I have to get you before Caesar because I'm fulfilling something in Rome that I told Daniel about back in the day." Because God had given Paul a purpose, He promised to get him through his storm.

You see, when you strive to be within God's will, He'll guide and protect you, and He'll keep you on track. When you sincerely try to live in a way that is holy and pleasing to the Lord, He'll bring you through your storm to your destiny.

Do You Believe God?

At the end of our selected text, Paul says, "I believe God, that it shall be even as it was told me" (Acts 27:25). Paul doesn't wait until after the storm has ended to place his trust in God—he proclaims his faith in the Lord, even as the nor'easter rages. In the same way you should learn to say, "I believe God will see me through every struggle"—no matter what your circumstances look like.

Thank God for sunshine. Thank Him for rain. Thank Him for appointments. Thank Him for disappointments. Trust that God will work out your life for your good according to His purposes.

Now, I need to pause here because sometimes people use the expression "I trust God" euphemistically. In today's American society we're often taught that if we "follow God," He'll bless us with a lot of stuff. Listen, when I say that God has a purpose for your life, I don't mean that He's going to give you earthly prosperity. Just because you say a couple "Give me this and that" prayers doesn't mean He'll work out your life according to your plans.

> *If God said it, you can believe that He's going to do it.*

God is not your personal wish-granting genie. You can't believe God to do things He never told you He'd do. For example, if you see someone who looks like your next boyfriend or girlfriend and start believing God will bring you together even though He hasn't given you any word about that person, it's not going to work out. Wish all you want— God is only going to give you what He has for you and no more. On the flipside, if God *said* it, you can believe that He's going to *do* it.

It doesn't matter who agrees or disagrees with you, because if God is for you, no one can stand against you. The only questions you need to ask are: "Lord, am I in Your will?

Am I following You the way I should? Am I living where You want me to live? Am I saying what You want me to say? Am I going where You've called me to go?"

Storm clouds may roll in, and strong winds may blow, but you have a Savior. Because Jesus died on the cross at Calvary, you are going to be all right. He was buried, but then, early Sunday morning, He arose in all His power. Because He got up, you have hope. Because He got up, you are going to make it. You can trust your entire being to Christ and His purposes.

Even if your boat has to get smashed up, God will work all things to your good. He will take care of you and give you joy. Ask God to reveal His purpose for you. Tell Him: "I believe You love me. I believe You'll guide me, hold me, protect me and teach me. I believe that—no matter what problems I face—You are able. I believe it's going to be all right."

It's time to believe God.

Discussion Questions:

1. What's your family background? What can your ancestors teach you—either through positive or negative examples—about hope, faith, love and trust (in God)?

2. If life isn't about "pie in the sky by and by" but about "hams and yams where I am," what can you do to make an impact for Christ in your own community? How does *living* for Christ differ from being a Christian who is just waiting to go to heaven?

3. Have other people ever gotten you into trouble? How did you react? What did you learn from the experience?

How might the outcome have been different if you had turned the entire situation over to Christ?

4. Have you ever had something taken away from you because you were disobedient? How did you react? What was the long-term impact?

Action Point: Get connected with other Christians who can encourage you to believe God. Claim the promises of God given to us in His Word, the Bible, over your own life.

4

ANIMALS AND ANGELS

And he was there in the wilderness forty days, tempted of Satan; and was with the wild beasts; and the angels ministered unto him. Mark 1:13

January came in kind of sour for me. I was having medical and family problems, and my perspective got a little warped. Then I dropped a weight on my toe at the gym and was stuck wearing this ridiculous little bootie. It was all-around bad news, and I got myself so worked up that I decided my entire year was shot.

I'd accepted that I was just going to have "one of those years"—until I got a wake-up call in the form of two mission trips: one to Uganda and the other to the lower ninth ward of New Orleans.

Those experiences put my life into a broader perspective. I realized that when I stopped being so self-focused, I actually had very little to gripe about. I wanted to complain, but I found that I didn't have much of a reason. I started singing "I'm Not Going to Complain": "I've got some good days. I've had some hills to climb. I've had some weary days and some lonely nights, but when I look around, and when I think things over, all of my good days outweigh all of my bad days, so I am not going to complain."

God's in control, so why should I be bitter when things don't work out my way? What right do I have to grumble and gripe? Not even Jesus had a problem-free life. He was

Trouble doesn't always hit your life because you messed up.

mocked for the truth He taught, denied by those who claimed to love Him, and cruelly crucified— even though He committed no crime! He was, by human standards, worse off than everyone

around Him, yet He was actually the Son of God, in whom the Father was well pleased (Mark 1:11).

Jesus' trials prove that trouble doesn't always hit your life because you messed up. You're not always being punished when things go wrong. In Mark 1:12 we learn that the Holy Spirit led Jesus into the wilderness immediately following His baptism. Did you catch that? Immediately after this heart-warming baptism and God's announcement that Jesus is His cherished Son, Christ gets driven out into the back country where Satan is waiting to tempt Him. Ouch.

If Jesus had to struggle, you can bet that you're also going to face physical and spiritual obstacles. As Christ's followers, we're going to face problems, but we should pray to God for His aid, because while Jesus had troubles, He also had spiritual comfort. Mark 1:13 tells us that Jesus was in the desert with wild animals during His temptation, yet angels came and ministered to Him. We too have to accept animals and angels in our lives.

"Animals and angels?" I can hear you ask. "What in the world are you talking about now, Alyn?" Well, "animals" are those very real physical problems you're going to have to deal with, and "angels" are the spiritual helpers God's going to send to help you through your trials. To find out how I know this and what it means for your life, stay with me. Read on.

Physically Dealing with "Animals"

Jesus' temptation shows us that some of the challenges we'll face as Christians are physical. Worldly struggles are going to factor into our spiritual situations, and we need to be prepared to deal with them.

Look at Mark 1:13: "And he [Jesus] was there in the wilderness forty days, tempted of Satan; and was with the wild beasts; and the angels ministered unto him." After forty days of fasting in the wilderness, you can imagine that Satan's first temptation—for Jesus to turn stones into bread—would be a serious one. Christ didn't only have to avoid spiritually giving into Satan to prove His deity—He also had to deal with His hunger and a growling stomach.

The devil and Jesus' appetite weren't the only things bothering Him out in the desert. After the first semi-colon in verse 13, we learn that Jesus was "with the wild beasts." We often tend to spiritualize Jesus to the point that His humanness is lost. Listen: Jesus lived in the physical world and functioned within a physical body. Jesus had to fight Satan's temptations while living in a hostile environment with wild animals.

Jesus wanted to focus on God in order to deal with the devil, yet He had to deal with very real problems called "wild beasts." While Jesus was trying to prepare for His ministry, harmful animals were getting all up in His face.

Picture it. Jesus is sitting there praying, and a snake slithers past. He's trying to get His praise on, and a lion roars.

You probably have an idea of what that feels like. Have you ever tried to get your life together but had to deal with

You don't need to fear your "animal" problems.

hissing, poisonous snakes like lying, back-stabbing friends? Have you ever tried to focus on God when your problems were roaring at you like lions? Just because you're a Christian doesn't mean you're exempt from facing physical issues—or "animals."

It's normal to have problems and to face animals—even when you're trying to do spiritually good things. It's not unfair for God to allow challenges in your life, because He uses them to grow you into a stronger person.

That said, you don't need to fear your "animal" problems. You don't see Jesus high-tailing it across the desert. He stuck it out because He knew that with God on His side, there wasn't anything to fear.

Let me see if I can make this plain. When I was in Uganda, I had to deal with some literal wild beasts. One night about twenty of us were staying out in the bush in this run-down house with no lights. Everything was fine until we heard something like footsteps or wings beating. We were in Africa, so we all got a little "scur'd."

We finally decided it was just bats, but that didn't fix our fear, because some of us had watched too much *Dracula*. Folk started covering up like something was going to come at their jugular. We ended up staying up all night, and let me just say I've never seen so many people play tic-tac-toe through the wee hours of the morning.

We were all worried over nothing. Our physical fear made our problem seem worse than it was. Unlike Jesus who stayed calm and collected in the desert, we got ourselves all worked up into thinking our "animal" problems were too great for us to handle.

Do you get what I'm saying? "Wild beasts"—or issues of the physical world—will only bother you if you let them. If you're on the side of righteousness, you don't have to focus on obstacles, because God will lead you around them. So don't get distracted from your pur-

"Dealing with animals" can sometimes mean navigating past others' negativity.

pose. Stick your chest out, throw your shoulders back and pick up your head, because "animals" have no power in your life.

Mentally and Emotionally Dealing with "Animals"

The "animals" you face might not only be physical problems—they can also be emotional. Although Jesus didn't have to deal with others' negative comments when He was alone in the wilderness, He did have to face them throughout His ministerial life. The fact is that "dealing with animals" can sometimes mean navigating past others' negativity.

You see, whenever you claim one of the eight thousand promises in the Bible, you'll find there's someone who doesn't want you to have it. Look at the Old Testament for an example. Every time you see the designation of the "land of milk and honey," you see that it's the land of the Hivities and the Jebusites and the Perizzites. Even though God had promised it to His people, others were camped out on the land and weren't about to just hand it over. They wanted to keep what they thought was theirs, and you'd better believe they had a list of criticisms to launch at the Israelites. God's people following God's will still had to deal with insults.

Life can wear you down when you start focusing on criticism. I often find myself mulling over everything that went wrong the previous day and allowing myself to be criticized by people who aren't even present. It's not worth it! We shouldn't give negativity a foothold in our lives.

My father gave me an analogy to help me deal with criticism. If you're not from a place where there are a lot of dogs roaming the streets, you might not quite get it, but I'll try to explain.

Dad told me, "Remember Alyn, dogs don't bark at parked cars." Did you get it? You see, I'm from Cleveland, Ohio where there are dogs all over the place. When you drive around, dogs run alongside your car and bark at it the entire way down the road. It might seem obvious, but they only make noise when they can chase you. You don't see any dogs sitting around barking at parked cars.

Sometimes folk will bark at you just because you're moving forward in God's purpose for your life. If you were parked in one stagnant place in your life, they'd leave you alone, but since you're in motion, they have something to say.

But there's an encouraging piece to this dog deal: dogs never leave their own blocks. When they bark at you, all you have to do is keep moving, because they aren't going to cross the street. They might bark when you're passing them, but if you keep going forward and don't get stuck listening to them, you'll be off that block before you know it. All you have to do to survive criticism is keep moving forward in God's plans. Life may get rough, and dogs may bark, but God is always good.

You're going to encounter obstacles of criticism, but you don't have to listen to all the disparaging remarks that come into your life. Just keep moving and seeking God's will, and He'll deal with the dogs. He's greater than any "animal."

God Will Send Spiritual Help

Anyway, let's get back to Jesus in the wilderness, because there's more to His story than a bunch of wild beasts. After the second semicolon in Mark 1:13, it says, "The angels ministered unto him." Christ was far from alone in the desert. God sent spiritual emissaries— or angels—to meet Jesus' spiritual need.

> *God will provide for you— even if it's right when you're convinced you can't handle your problem.*

In the same way, even if you have to deal with the devil and wild beasts, God will send His angels to be with you and minister to you. What a promise for your life!

Jesus had to deal with some sticky situations, but God saw Him through His struggles. God loves you in a similar way, and He'll provide for you—even if it's right when you're convinced you can't handle your problem any longer. He'll send angels just in the nick of time. You might go to bed thinking your problem is going to kill you tomorrow—only to wake up to find God sent an angel. God will answer your prayer when it needs answering.

The angels God sends are not just pretty, white, winged beings who sing up in the sky. Angelic messengers can also come in the form of humans—people God sends right when they're necessary.

I heard a story once of this poor woman who desperately needed money for food. Broke and feeling hungry, she began to pray at her window: "God, please, I need some food." On Monday she prayed, "God, I need food." On Tuesday she prayed, "God, I need food." On Wednesday she prayed, "God, I need food."

The "angels" God uses might surprise you.

There was an atheist next door to her who thought this looked like a great opportunity to show her God didn't exist. He thought, *I am really going to get this woman.* He ran down to the store, bought some food and left it outside her front door. The woman came out, saw the food and began to praise God: "Oh, Lord, thank You for providing this food!" When the man heard this, he came running out and said, "Ha! There is no God. I'm the one who put the food there!" The woman just smiled and responded, "No, you don't understand. God provided for me. He just used you to pay the bill."

The "angels" God uses might surprise you, but one way or another, He'll supply for your needs. God sends spiritual help—or "angels"—to keep us from getting discouraged by all the physical trials—or "animals"—in our day-to-day lives. It doesn't matter how dark your situation looks or how hard your life has been. When angels begin to work on you, you'll come out empowered on the other side of the struggle.

Emerging from the Desert

There's another thing that blows my mind about the story of Jesus' temptation. If you keep reading in Mark 1, Jesus goes straight from wandering in the wilderness to preaching in Galilee, teaching the Word in Nazareth, and healing and presenting the truth in Capernaum. The Bible says He astonished His audience by the power of His doctrine, because He spoke like no one they'd heard before (Luke 4:14–37).

Something stands out to me here. Jesus hadn't eaten for forty days. He had been tempted by the devil and had battled wild beasts, yet He has *power* when He speaks. Think about it. He should have looked pretty beaten down, but when

You *may be the angel.*

He preaches, no one is distracted by His appearance. Why not? Because they're focused on His word.

When you keep your eyes fixed on God, others will follow your gaze to find Him as well. What a testimony when others see past the marks of turmoil on your face to the peace of Christ!

You see, although you may need angels to minister to you in your struggles, when you reach the other side, you may be called to be an angel to others. It's not about you receiving and never giving—you have to do part of the work as well. Christ's economy says that you get what you give.

Since *you* may be the angel sometimes, you need to watch how you talk to people, how you act and how you open your heart to others. Sometimes holding a door, asking "Can I help you? Can I be there for you?" or just saying a warm "Hello!" can make all the difference in someone's life.

God has a funny way of working sometimes. He may use someone you thought was no good to bless you and then call you to help out someone you thought you couldn't stand. He may use you to minister to someone at the perfect moment. Learn to listen and respond. Don't let the fact that a person is of different race or gender or from a different culture keep you from lending a helping hand. Don't let the fact that you don't like someone keep you from praying for that person.

Loving others is the second greatest command after loving God—so do it! I know it's not easy to be an angel to others. I know it's not easy to move past the criticisms and physical obstacles in your life. But guess what? Jesus did it, and God wants to help you through.

Following Christ means you might end up in the middle of the wilderness with scary things all about you, but you won't be alone. You will emerge from those struggles with a new hope and a stronger faith.

Physical and spiritual struggles are both realities of life, but "animals" can't keep you down, and "angels" will only lift you up. Jesus already fought and won your spiritual battle, so don't get distracted by barking dogs. Just keep moving.

Discussion Questions:

1. What obstacles are in the way of your Christian walk? What things are you allowing to distance you from God? Ask the Lord to make His direction for your life clear so you aren't troubled and sidetracked by such things.

2. Can you think of some "angels" God has sent to help you along the way? Why does it matter that, while God allows animals, He also sends angels?

3. Do you ever criticize yourself more than you should? How can you maintain a biblical self-perspective to keep

from being beaten down by others' harmful words?

4. Philippians 4:6 says, "Do not be anxious about anything, but in everything, by prayer and petition, with thanksgiving, present your requests to God" (NIV). Do you ever find yourself complaining about your life? What can you do to change your perspective and give God total control?

Action Point: Think of a way to be an "angel" to someone near you—and then do it!

5

RUNNING TO GOD WHEN LIFE GETS WEIRD

How long wilt thou forget me, O LORD? for ever? how long wilt thou hide thy face from me?
How long shall I take counsel in my soul, having sorrow in my heart daily? how long shall mine enemy be exalted over me?
Consider and hear me, O LORD my God: lighten mine eyes, lest I sleep the sleep of death;
Lest mine enemy say, I have prevailed against him; and those that trouble me rejoice when I am moved.
But I have trusted in thy mercy; my heart shall rejoice in thy salvation.
I will sing unto the LORD, because he hath dealt bountifully with me.   Psalm 13:1–6

Have you ever felt like your life had been turned upside down? "What do I do now?" you might have cried.

How do you deal with moments when everything seems to be coming back to bite you? What do you do when you want to cry out, "Why *me*, God?!"

While we don't want to blame God for our problems, we also don't believe we should have to struggle. Some biblical scholars refer to this problem as wrestling with theodicy. Basically, we desire to defend God's goodness in light of the evil of the world. We question: "How can I maintain my belief in the omnipotence, omniscience and omnipresence of God despite all of the messed up stuff that's happening to me?"

Romans 8:28 comes to the rescue to help answer our theodicy questions: "All things work together for good to them that love God, to them who are the called according to his purpose." Everything that seems so negative to you now is going to work out for your good. You may have to suffer, but God will bring you through.

God will work through your struggle, but He might do it in a way that seems strange.

Now, while it's true that God will work out your life according to His purpose, that doesn't mean He's going to work out your life according to *your* plans. God will work through your struggle with you, but He might do it in a way that seems strange.

Sometimes it can be difficult to maintain your testimony of hope when your life involves pain, because there is a theology in the church today that says that if you "love God"—in the sense that you go to church and say your prayers—you will be blessed with health, riches and happiness. While this "prosperity gospel" may sound good, God's blessings are not tied to earthly rewards.

Say you get into an accident and walk away without a scratch and testify that this is because the Lord loves you, but I get into an accident and am paralyzed. You run around talking about how good God is, but I'm stuck like this for the rest of my life. How do I deal with why God didn't fix it for me? Does it mean I failed to be "Christian enough"?

What am I missing? You see, God's purposes for us are not wrapped up in our physical needs. He gives and takes away to grow us in our faith, and even as Christians, we have to learn to deal with the good and the bad.

God never promised the Christian walk would be easy. In fact, He said just the opposite—following Christ is *difficult*. Look at the disciples. They weren't multi-millionaires who were waited on hand and foot. They didn't receive earthly

> *The disciples served—and most of them lived hard lives and died difficult deaths because of it.*

riches. Instead, they served—and most of them lived hard lives and died difficult deaths because of it. But guess what? Their reward in heaven is great.

We need to accept that God doesn't always do things the way we want them done. He uses trials to humble and strengthen us. He doesn't pick favorites or give out door prizes. Even if you're a good person, you might have to deal with some bad situations.

The truth of the matter is that when life feels wrong, we don't need material blessings. Riches aren't going to fix our problems. Instead, we need to trust that a Person who deeply loves us—Jesus Christ—is working out our lives for ultimate good.

Sometimes It's Just Your Turn

It's easy in theory to say that God has our lives under control, but it can be difficult to accept His "blessings" when they come in the form of a struggle. But the reality is that even if you're a tongues-talking super saint who tithes and never misses a day of church, your world can still be suddenly turned upside down. You're going to have to deal with issues whether or not you do anything to cause trouble. Christian or not, sometimes your number just comes up.

In Psalm 13 David is struggling with a dry season in his faith and wondering where God went. God hadn't left David—He was just allowing him to experience a time of struggling. David, however, wrestled with feeling alone and cried out "How long will this last?"

When I was writing this chapter, I gained some insight into where David was coming from. He told me: "Alyn, I know you need to understand this text, so let me explain. You see, life has been rough for me since I decided to take on Goliath. My family got angry with me, because I wasn't scared. When God took my father-in-law Saul's anointing and gave it to me, Saul turned on me too. At that point everything seemed to be falling apart. Stuff was coming from my family *and* from my foes. People didn't like me just because I was favored. To top it all off, I was young and far from perfect, so I was getting grief from everyone while trying to deal with my own faults and failings."

David felt like God had gone on vacation when his enemies were upon him. In Psalm 13 he didn't know how God was going to work things out, so he cried, "How long are You going to let this happen?!" David felt like God wasn't doing what He had done in the past.

Like David, you sometimes have to accept that upsetting things happen, and God isn't going to immediately fix them. This doesn't mean that God is angry with you. Even when life feels wrong, remember that God has a deeper design than you can understand.

Run to God

You may not like what David says in the text, but you have to love what he does. When it looks like everything is going wrong in his life and like his enemies are winning, he doesn't turn away from God and throw a pity party. Instead, he goes to the Lord in prayer: "How long wilt Thou forget me, O LORD? . . .

> *The only One who is going to get you out of whatever you're in is God.*

Consider and hear me, O LORD my God" (Ps. 13:1, 3). Even if what David says seems impious, he at least acknowledges that God is real and has the answer.

Listen: every time weird stuff happens in your life, you can't just run back to what you used to be and what you used to do before you knew Christ. That's exactly what the devil wants you to do.

So what should you do? Run straight to God and be in His presence. Tell Him how you're feeling, and pray for His purposes to be made clear to you. You see, the only One who is going to get you out of whatever you're in is God. The only One who can keep you going on the right track is God. The only One who can fix your problems, if they're going to be fixed, is God. Don't bother turning to anything or anyone else, because God is the one and only answer.

Get Real with God

David shows us that we need to turn to the Lord, but when he talks to God, the passage gets sticky. Why do we start feeling some theological anxiety when David addresses God? Because David asks a question that makes us wonder whether the word from this man's mouth is supposed to be the Word of God to us. I mean, why are the words, "How long wilt Thou forget me, O God?" even in my Bible?

I feel like saying, "Whoa, David. You have some audacity to project onto God an anthropomorphic personality—and a negative one at that!" And if you keep reading, you see that David isn't done demanding answers. He questions: "God, why aren't You listening?" and "God, why are You letting this happen?" Verses 3 and 4 read: "Hear me, O LORD . . . Lest mine enemy say, I have prevailed against him; and those that trouble me rejoice when I am moved." In other words, "Are You just going to sit back and let these guys win? Are You going to let them make me into a laughing-stock?" David questions the motives of the God of the universe, because they don't seem to align with what *he* thinks is best. I don't know about you, but I'm not a fan of this *me me me* theology.

> *You don't have a* religion—*you have a* relationship *with God.*

Maybe I'm being too hard on David though, because what he does isn't necessarily wrong. Allow me to explain— God wants us to tell Him what's really on our minds. David does this in the psalms, which were written to help us understand that God can handle every possible human emotion. Because God deeply cares about us, He wants us to come to Him with our doubts as well as with our praise.

You see, you don't have a *religion*—you have a *relationship* with God. In a religion you have to get everything right. You have to say everything correctly and follow all the rules. In a relationship, however, you can say whatever is on your mind to the other person, and you can talk it out until you get where you need to be.

Think about one of your close, trustworthy friends. What is conversation like with that person? Easy? When you're in a real, loving relationship with someone, you can tell that person anything and everything. While you may disagree for a while, your problems will be resolved by the time you're done talking. It's basically the same way with God. When you run to God and acknowledge your relationship with Him, He'll allow you to have a real conversation with Him.

Does David's situation make more sense now? David's whining is not authoritative; he simply spills his heart's troubles out before the Lord. You too can tell God how you're truly feeling. He loves you and wants to meet you in your time of need in order to turn your pain into praise. He'll allow you to be wrong with Him until He can get right with you.

Let's look at this "being real" with God concept from another angle. When I think of what a real, honest relationship looks like, I think of kids, because they say what they think, and they do what they feel like doing.

I used to love when my nephew Quinn would come over, because there wasn't anything complicated about the way he operated. He'd knock, say hi, come in and we'd play.

When it was time to go, however, Quinn would go crazy. His mother would say, "Pack up your toys," and he would cry, "Noooooooo!" Now Robin, his mom, is about the chillest woman on the planet. She never loses her cool. While Quinn was hollering and objecting, she'd be collecting his toys and getting his coat. While he was screaming,

"Noooooo, Mommy!" she'd be picking him up, hugging him and kissing him to try to calm him down. Even when he kept crying "No, no, no, noooo!" she'd keep smiling as if to say she loved him and knew what was best for him.

> *Sometimes we kick and fight against God. He holds us, wraps us in His arms and carries us to His house where we can find real rest.*

What would always blow my mind is that even though he might be fighting and yelling when he left, Robin would always call when they got about half a mile from our house to say that Quinn had calmed down and was already asleep.

Do you see where I'm going with this? Sometimes we too fight and kick against God. He might not like it, but He holds us, wraps us in His arms and carries us to His house where we can find real rest. Even though God might not change the fact that we don't like what's going on, we can rest assured that it'll be all right. We can be real with Him about how we're feeling—even if that means yelling at the top of our lungs until we finally see His purpose.

This is what David recognizes in the text. This is how we get from verse 4 to verse 5. David starts out complaining and worrying that his enemies are going to get the best of him. Then it's as if someone took a page from another psalm and pasted it on top of Psalm 13. David goes from shaking his fist to being as malleable as butter. Even though God didn't change his situation, David recognized it was going to be all right. He writes: "But I have trusted in Thy mercy; my heart shall rejoice in Thy salvation."

What happened here? What changed? Not enough time

passed between these verses for anything to have changed externally. David's problems and enemies were still real, but he remembered the promises of the Lord. David got real with God, and God met him in his complaint and changed him internally.

Thank God for Your Future!

If you fast-forward to the end of our text, you'll see that David got more than a one-time perspective shift. He not only decided to trust God in the moment but to believe Him to secure his future.

Now, I don't mean to get grammatical on you, but follow me for a minute, because David messes me up in verse 6 when he says, "I will sing unto the LORD, because he hath dealt bountifully with me." You see, this line is in what some biblical scholars call the "prophetic perfect tense." The prophetic perfect is used when someone is affirming something in the future as if it already happened in the past because they're certain that it's going to come to pass. So David is saying that he *will sing* (future tense) because the Lord *hath dealt* (past tense) with him bountifully.

David says, "It's not that confusing guys. I'm talking about what God is going to do; I'm just talking about it as if He has already done it. Why? Because I know that it's going to be all right. I don't need Him to fix it right now, since I know He has it under control and will work it out in His time." Does it make sense now?

God doesn't always fix things the way we think they should be fixed. He doesn't have to do what we want Him to do to fulfill His will. David knows he might still have enemies and he might still have problems, but if God addresses the situation according to His will, everything will be all right.

Have you ever been frustrated when God kept saying no to your prayer only to discover that was the best thing for you at the time? Maybe you would have ended up in the wrong place with the wrong person had you gotten what you asked for; instead, God shook up your life in order to give you what you needed.

God's purpose is not hindered by the limitations of your thinking.

You may be of the opinion that God can't handle or doesn't want to deal with your questions. Well, I have news for you: God's purpose is not hindered by the limitations of your thinking. He wants you to go to Him in prayer and tell Him what's really on your mind, because when you open yourself to Him, He can get into your situation.

Life might not *feel* all right, but it *is* all right. In other words, you might not like what's going on in your life, but when God gets into it—even if the reality of life doesn't change—you can be renewed on the inside and experience real transformation.

God has proven Himself throughout history, so start praising Him as if He has already done the work in your life. Praise Him because you know it's going to work out. Hebrews 13:8 says, "Jesus Christ [is] the same yesterday, and today, and forever." His promises for the past are the same as His promises for the future. Praise Him like you've already seen the end of your trials.

Sometimes life gets weird and feels strange to us, but we need to trust the Lord at *all* times. Think about the struggles of some biblical characters. Being in a lion's den probably felt weird to Daniel, but the Lord showed up and shut the lions' mouths. It's strange that Shadrach, Meshach and Abednego weren't burned in the fire, but that's because the Lord was in the fire with them. It was painful to be hanged on the

If God said "it is so," then you need to act like it's so, even if it isn't so, until it becomes so.

Calvary cross, but Jesus never forgot His purpose. The onlookers probably thought it was weird when the King wore a crown of thorns and was placed in the grave. But do you know the rest of the story? Early Sunday morning, Jesus Christ got up with all power in His hands. It went from *weird* to *wonderful.*

God took Jesus from weird to wonderful, so He'll lead you out of wherever you are right now to where you're meant to be. If God said "it is so," then you need to act like it's so, even if it isn't so, until it becomes so. Whew!

If life gets weird and it seems like your enemies are winning and you can't figure it out, that's all right. You know who's in control. Maybe God wants to do something new in your life, and you need to go through some pain to be prepared.

I don't know where you are right now. I don't know if you're hurting and feel like David in verse 4, but you need to trust the Lord. Tell Him that you'll never make it without Him. Maybe it's your turn for a hard season, but you have hope. Run to God.

Discussion Questions:

1. What does "all things work together for good to them
   that love God, to them who are the called according to
   his purpose" mean to you? How does this impact the
   way you live?

2. To get David's backstory, read First Samuel 17. Have
   you ever faced a Goliath (a big, seemingly unconquer-
   able problem) in your life? What was it? Did you run to
   God or run away? What were the consequences of your
   actions?

3. Think about the relationship you have with your closest
   friend. What defines it? What would it mean to make
   your relationship with God the same?

4. Psalm 3:5–6 tells us, "Trust in the LORD with all thine
   heart; and lean not unto thine own understanding. In
   all thy ways acknowledge him, and he shall direct thy
   paths." Are you trying to lead your own life? What might
   you be holding back from God? What would it look like
   to turn everything over to His control?

Action Point: Read God's promise to the Israelite exiles in
Jeremiah 29:11–14. Call out to God and dedicate yourself
to seeking His will. Ask God to take your life from weird to
wonderful through the refreshing power of His Holy Spirit.

6

GOD WILL TAKE CARE OF YOU

The word of the LORD came unto [Elijah], saying, Get thee hence, and turn thee eastward, and hide thyself by the brook Cherith, that is before Jordan. And it shall be, that thou shalt drink of the brook; and I have commanded the ravens to feed thee there. So he went and did according unto the word of the LORD . . . And it came to pass after a while, that the brook dried up, because there had been no rain in the land.

And the word of the LORD came unto him, saying, Arise, get thee to Zarephath, which belongeth to Zidon, and dwell there: behold, I have commanded a widow woman there to sustain thee. So he arose and went to Zarephath. 1 Kings 17:2–10

It was the best of times, it was the worst of times," writes Charles Dickens in *A Tale of Two Cities*. We like this familiar quote, because although it seems contradictory, it rings true. The good and the bad tend to go together—our best moments often come from maintaining hope through the worst.

I live in Philadelphia, and I find Dickens's quote really nails our city's current economic situation. Philly's work force investment board recently put out a pamphlet stating the city is experiencing an economic boom: neighborhoods are being revitalized, property values are going up and the job market is strengthening. That said, despite the fact that Philadelphia is the buckle on the money belt between New York City and Washington D.C., it has one of the highest rates of people living at or below the poverty line in America's top ten cities. Philadelphia is surrounded by top tier universities, yet only 20 percent of its residents have a Bachelor's Degree. This used to be a blue collar city with jobs for low-skilled workers, but now you can't get hired without a specific knowledge set. The dichotomy between those with money and formal education versus those who are impoverished and unschooled is disconcerting. The best off and the worst off don't mix. Nothing balances. It's the best and the worst of times—but you only get to pick one.

> *You have to face the worst realities of the world in the light of the best promises of God.*

As Christians however, we don't have to stress about the world's issues. Jesus told His disciples to leave their goods and their friends behind, take up their crosses and follow Him (Matt. 16:24). We should do the same. If we follow Christ, He'll provide what we need, and if we listen to God's commands, He'll bless us according to His purposes.

Nothing can separate us from the love of God. The economy may struggle, but God will take care of His people. We don't have to worry about trouble winning in our lives, because in Jesus' name, we have victory. With Christ in our lives, nothing is ever the worst, because God loves us and desires to work all things to our *best.* No matter what your external circumstances look like, the Lord will take care of you.

Now, I'm not presenting an escapist mentality. I'm not telling you to just sit around waiting for God to fix things. I'm not telling you to hide out and worship in your church, basking in your religiosity until Jesus' Second Coming. Instead, you have to face the worst realities of the world in the light of the best promises of God. You have to get off of your "blessed assurance" to go where God's telling you to go and to do what He has called you to do. When you trust Him, He'll lead you through every struggle.

I want to look at the prophet Elijah, because he didn't worry about anything in his life. Elijah relied on God to take care of him, and guess what? God did. If you put your faith in Him, God will take care of you as well.

Living in a Land of Unbelief

We're going to be looking at a couple of stories in Kings 17:1–15 that show Elijah trusting God and God providing for Elijah. Before diving into the text, however, I want to give some background information. Elijah lived in a messed up place. The people who lived around him worshiped Baal instead of the Lord. Although they'd been blessed by God, they thanked Baal. In spite of the fact that God had sustained them, they weren't giving Him any credit.

Their blatant disobedience led to a drought. God recognized His people weren't following Him, so He held back the rain. No matter how much the people prayed to Baal, he couldn't irrigate their crops when they ran out of water. Without crops, the people couldn't keep animals. Without animals, they couldn't eat. Without eating, they'd lose their strength and die—all because God wasn't going to let it rain until they returned to Him.

Elijah never forgot who God was, but he lived with people who had. Since he was in a city whose leaders had messed up, he had to deal with the physical realities of God's judgment. Despite Elijah's faithfulness and devotion to the Lord, he still had to deal with the drought.

Are you following? You may not have personally been unfaithful to God, but if you're living in an unfaithful context, the realities of life are going to hit you as well. It's possible that you might have to deal with some of the fallout from others' choices.

> *Since Elijah was in a city whose leaders had messed up, he had to deal with the physical realities of God's judgment.*

Because sin is in the world, it may stop by your house for a visit. Trouble isn't going to pass you by just because you're a super saint. The Bible tells us the Lord "maketh his sun to rise on the evil and on the good, and sendeth rain on the just and on the unjust" (Matt. 5:45). Good and bad experiences happen to "good" and "bad" people. Even as a pastor, I don't assume that every day is going to be easy. Just because I have on a nice suit and go to church doesn't mean I'm safe from everything crashing down around me.

All of that said, the Lord takes care of His own. Yes, the drought is an issue, but the Lord doesn't leave Elijah to shrivel up in the heat. Elijah isn't just left to die.

What happens in the text after Elijah makes the Lord's pronouncement to Ahab blows my mind. It shows that God does not forget those who follow Him—even when everyone else is missing the message. God commands Elijah to go down to the brook Cherith where ravens had been commanded to feed him. Because Elijah trusted the Lord, the Lord provided for his needs.

You may be caught up in a sinful place and may have some sin of your own, but God has not abandoned you. I don't know what happened in your house last night or what's going on in your neighborhood, but God will provide for you.

Elijah had to keep trusting and keep following.

He desires to take care of you and to restore you to the person He created you to be.

You might have to deal with some bad times simply because you live in a fallen world, but if you trust God, He'll keep you alive and secure. He will take care of you.

Are You Following God?

Aside from the fact that Elijah gets carry-out delivered by birds, there's something else that seems strange about the way God works. Let's look at it. God says, "Hey, Elijah, I know you have to deal with this drought, but no worries—some birds are going to hook you up with food. Here's what you need to do: head on down to Cherith."

Did you catch it? God doesn't just say, "Thanks for doing what I told you to do Elijah," and make a banquet table appear out of thin air. Instead, He sends Elijah to a brook. God says, "I need you to go to the brook, Elijah. If you're not there, you're not going to get fed. The ravens aren't going to go door to door to find you." Elijah can't just kick back and relax after delivering God's message; he has to keep trusting and to keep following. Only by going to Cherith can Elijah receive his blessing.

God tells Elijah to go to the brook, to stay at the brook, to be obedient to what he has been told. Even though there is a drought in the land, God promises to take care of Elijah if Elijah takes the first step of trusting Him and seeking His Spirit. You see, sometimes when you want God to provide for you, you have to move your feet. You may be wondering why everything's wrong and why you aren't seeing any provision in your life. Well, maybe you're fighting the next step in your life. Are you ready to follow where God calls you to go? There and there alone will you receive your blessing.

If you run away from where God has told you to be, how do you expect to receive His blessings?

Let me see if I can clarify what I'm saying. Do you know what a timing pattern in football is? Basically, instead of throwing the ball to the receiver, the quarterback throws the ball to a pre-determined point on the field where the receiver runs as soon as the ball is in the air. When the quarterback and receiver are in sync, it's an extremely difficult play to defend against. The quarterback doesn't have to wait for a player to get open—he can throw the ball and, ideally, trust the receiver to get where he needs to be.

Do you see the connection? God knows the play. He's throwing the ball so everything will fall into place correctly and you can run the entire way to the end zone. This doesn't work very well, however, if you don't run to where you're supposed to be. If you cut in the opposite direction, how do you expect to catch the football? If you run away from where God has told you to be, how do you expect to receive His blessings?

Whatever you're going through, you have one thing to ask yourself: Am I in the will of God? Am I there? God never promised to provide for you if you weren't living according to His will. His grace and mercy are sufficient, but you have to be willing to go where He's called you, because that's where He'll sustain you.

God Provides in Strange Ways

Let's recap. Elijah's culture wasn't worshiping God, so God got angry. God sent a drought, but Elijah listened to God, so God provided for him. Because Elijah went where God sent him, he was sustained. This all makes sense, but it still seems like God works in funny ways.

Sometimes God uses our difficulties and our enemies to bless us.

Read First Kings 17:6: "The ravens brought him bread and flesh in the morning, and bread and flesh in the evening." I don't know about you, but I have to ask, why ravens?

God's use of ravens is interesting. Think about it: the land is experiencing a drought, so the animals are all probably pretty hungry. Ravens eat meat, yet they're the ones carrying food to Elijah. When I was in seminary, those who didn't believe miracles could happen tried to discredit the fact that ravens brought the food, because it was too hard to believe that the birds would give up their food for some hungry man. You see, sometimes God brings help from strange places.

Elijah should have had to fight the ravens for their food. Instead, the ravens that ought to have hurt him, helped him. Something that should have pushed him down, helped him up.

When trouble comes, folk you thought you could count on will leave you and sell you out. You just have to thank God for the ravens in your life. The folk you think are trying to hurt you might end up helping you. The folk you think are trying to take from you might give to you.

Sometimes God uses our difficulties and our enemies to bless us. Maybe you got laid off, but it gave you the impetus to start your own business. Maybe you missed your train, but it gave you more time to build a relationship. Maybe someone talked about you behind your back, but it led to the right person knowing your name at the right time. Ravens are things that help you rise above your problems when they should have hurt you.

Now, being provided for may sound good, but remember that being fed by ravens isn't exactly glamorous. In fact, it's kind of gross. God sustains Elijah, but He doesn't serve up filet mignon on a silver platter.

When I say God will provide, I don't mean that He'll hook you up with a mansion, a limousine and a swimming pool full of money. I'm not telling you God is going to get you a six-figure income no matter what kind of work experience and education you have, because that'd be a lie. Sometimes you have to work—"meet God halfway," so to speak—to succeed. You might say, "Listen, Pastor Waller, you don't know my family's structure! You don't understand. I can't afford to send my children to college, and even if I could, not every child can make it in an academic environment. I can't get a job! I can't!" I hear you, but just fill out the application, go to the interview, do what you can. You need to prepare yourself for the future, trusting that—even if He does it in a strange way—God will meet your needs.

Put God First!

Although God will sustain you when you follow Him, things might get a little rough. At the beginning of Elijah's adventure, there was a drought. Elijah listened to the Lord and went to Cherith where he had food and water, and everything was all right. Then just when

Some things meant for your survival aren't going to last your lifetime.

things were looking up for Elijah, his brook dried up. Talk about frustrating!

In verse 7 Cherith gives up the ghost, and Elijah is stuck sitting by a desiccated brook bed. This is one of those biblical moments that make me say, "What?!" To me, it would have made sense for God to allow the brook to dry up if Elijah had disobeyed Him or gone to the wrong place, but that wasn't the case. God *sent* him to Cherith, and then it dried up! I wonder if Elijah questioned, "God, did You know when You sent me here that this brook wasn't going to sustain me forever?"

There's a lesson to be learned from Elijah's seeming misfortune. You need to understand that some things meant for your survival aren't going to last your lifetime. God may have led you to somewhere to fulfill a specific purpose, and once you've completed your function, that place may dry up.

Have you ever had a relationship dry up on you? Have you ever had a church dry up on you? Have you ever had a job dry up on you? Maybe nothing went wrong—maybe you'd simply fulfilled your purpose in those places and with those people, and it was time to move on.

The important thing is that the story doesn't end with

Elijah dying of thirst. Right after the brook goes dry as a bone, the Lord tells Elijah that He has prepared a widow to sustain him. The Lord takes Elijah from a place of mere survival and brings him to a new place of sustenance. At the brook, dirty birds brought Elijah raw meat and bread, but God sends him to a woman who can bake some cake. Hallelujah! God doesn't just leave Elijah to die, so we can trust that He'll lead us through our dry seasons as well.

Now, Elijah listens to God's call and goes to the widow's house, but when he shows up, she doesn't seem to know what's going on. God said He had commanded a widow to sustain Elijah, but she didn't have an all-you-can-eat buffet waiting. God may have prepared her heart, but Elijah had to *keep* trusting. He had to humble himself and ask a poor woman to provide for him—knowing God would bless her if she obeyed.

Look at the text. Elijah says, "Give me some food," and the widow says, "But I don't really have much. I just have a little meal and a little oil—only enough for a hoecake." Now, you probably don't know what a hoecake is because most people don't make biscuits from scratch anymore. Instead, you just pop the can, pull out the biscuits and stick 'em on a cookie sheet. My grandma, however, used to make hoecakes by lumping all of the scrapings left over from biscuits together. That strange-looking loaf was all the widow had left.

Now, if I were Elijah, I would have kept on moving, saying, "Oops, sorry! I must have the wrong house. God probably meant to send me to a widow who could make some real food." But Elijah remembers what the Lord told him, and he is confident in that purpose. As a prophet of God in a place of God's priority, Elijah tells the woman, "Listen, if you want to be taken care of, then listen to me. Before you eat anything, break some off for me. I know you don't have a lot, but if you prioritize God with what you have, God will not let you run out."

Pay attention to what happens. When the widow gives to Elijah, she doesn't run out of food and starve to death. Instead, her barrel

The Lord will bring you from survival to sustenance.

is filled to overflowing. Because she obeys, both her family and Elijah are provided for.

You see, life may present multiple struggles, but that just means that God will bring multiple provisions. When the widow trusted, she was blessed. When Elijah followed God's leading first to Cherith and then to the widow's home, he was rewarded for his faith and trust. Although neither of these actions was easy, they led to blessings. Like Elijah and the widow, you need to listen for God's command, follow His call and trust Him to take care of you.

God knows where you are and what you need in life. Sure, you may get worried about the economy. You may have concerns about your brothers and sisters. But know that if you do what God has called you to do, then He'll watch over you.

Do you hear what I'm saying? You don't have to be content with your situation; you just have to trust God through it. No matter how dry the brook gets or how much you want to throw up your hands and cry, "This is for the birds!" God has you. Declare: "Jesus knows what's best for me even though my weary eyes can't see."

Every once in a while, your brook might dry up, but that's okay, because it means God's going to release a river. When He dries up a place, He's getting ready to lead you to a palace. All you have to do is move forward saying, "*Hasta luego*, dried up brook. God is taking me from a flock of dirty birds to a widow who can cook." Then praise the Lord and give Him the glory for bringing you from survival to sustenance.

You may be saying, "Preacher, my brook has dried up, and I'm tired of trying to get by with half-dead birds. I'm ready to change. I'm ready to have my life transformed and to live wholly for the Lord. I want to listen and respond when He calls." Listen: there's no time like the present to give your life to Christ.

Through the best of times and worst of times, there is one constant: the Lord your God will take care of you.

Discussion Questions:

1. What "security"—be it financial, relational or personal—might you have to leave behind to whole-heartedly follow Jesus?

2. Have you ever run into problems because of your environment? What was God teaching you through those difficulties?

3. Has God ever dried up a brook on you, so to speak? What was your reaction? What parts of your life or which emotions do you still need to turn over to Him? What would it look like to fully trust in His provision over your own abilities?

4. Do you feel like you're struggling to survive with a mea-
   ger supply for your physical, emotional and spiritual
   needs? Claim God's transforming power!

Action Point: Ask a mature Christian you know about how
God has led him/her through struggles. (You can also ask
him/her to pray for you as you learn to obey God's call!)

7

Lessons from the Night

For his anger endureth but a moment; in his favour is life: weeping may endure for a night, but joy cometh in the morning.
Psalm 30:5

Have you ever cried yourself to sleep? In those moments it's easy to feel like everything is wrong and to believe you're never going to escape. Then somehow you make it through the pain and promise yourself you'll never get into the same situation again.

Seasons like these are a fact of life; everyone experiences this ebb and flow between sorrow and joy, struggling and rejoicing. Just as the natural world has summer, fall, winter and spring, you will have sunny moments and dry periods. Unfortunately, life has a way of changing when you least expect it. You may be having an awful day when someone blesses you with a word of encouragement, or you may be on top of the world when life throws you a disastrous curveball.

Life includes both good and bad times, and you need to be ready and thankful for each new phase. You should accept dark days because, in His own time, the Lord will return you to light and joy. You'll enjoy a new, stronger happiness—refined by sorrow. Even when you're going through a rough time, you can trust Jesus to be your calming constant. While it can be easy to lose hope, focus on struggles and dark seasons and miss the coming dawn, remember: there is a time for everything, and no season lasts forever.

There's a song on my CD *With His Permission* called "Seasons" that discusses enduring trials and having your faithfulness tested by a difficult time yet trusting Jesus to see

> *God works in the calm and quiet of night.*

you through. It says, "When you wish the pain would fade away but it lingers for another day, it's just a season. Although seasons may change, Jesus will always stay the same." I have to admit that when Howard Kennedy, the young man who wrote this song, first gave it to me, I didn't want to sing it. I didn't want to let those words come out of my mouth. I was afraid that if I told God I'd trust Him no matter what He threw at me, a night season might come my way. I listened to other artists singing about positive seasons of growth and plentiful harvests, and I decided I'd rather do a song about a season of plenty than about suffering. I didn't want to sing about lingering pain; I wanted to praise God for blessings.

I finally realized that it's silly to resist "night seasons." They're a natural part of each person's faith life, and there is a lot to be gained from these dark periods.

God Works in Night Seasons

Dark periods in our life often get a bad rap, but the truth is that God often works in the calm and quiet of night. David knew what it was like to keep going and keep trusting— even when everything seemed to be falling apart. In Psalm

30:5 he writes, "weeping may endure for a night, but joy cometh in the morning." You see, he trusted the Lord to teach him how to persevere and learn through his night. David saw the flipside of pain and trusted God's ability to turn his sorrow into joy.

Psalm 30 is an example of David's willingness to quiet himself before the Lord and to wait for the morning's joy. He knew what it meant to write, "[The Lord] maketh me to lie down in green pastures" (Ps. 23:2). You see, we're often quick to focus on the green pastures in this verse and to skip right past the "He maketh me" part. Have you ever thought about what it means to be made to lie down? In other words, you should be still, but you refuse to be still, so God's going to make you be still. He's going to make you quiet down and listen during your night season.

God's going to make you quiet down and listen during your night season.

Night seasons come for a reason, even if you don't immediately recognize their purpose. My brother died when I was in college, and the pain of losing him made it impossible to concentrate on my studies and to seek out "the college experience." Now, I would never say that God killed my brother, but it was in the dark season of his death that my heart was opened to hear God speaking in a way I never would have heard Him when I was out partying. Through this tragic experience God met me in my quiet place, took hold of my heart and called me into the ministry. Even in my pain, God showed me His goodness.

David had a similar experience of finding God in his

period of weeping. Although David was close to God when life was good, he experienced what it meant to really cry out to God when everything fell apart and he was surrounded by people who wished him harm. God used David's night season to draw him closer.

But why did David need to struggle with anything in the first place? He was a man of God, right? Well, although David trusted God, following the Lord wasn't always easy for him. In Psalm 30:6 we find David in need of a reality check and a pride check. He says, "In my prosperity, I shall never be moved." When you unpack that language, what he's basically saying is that only when he has it going on—when everything feels right—does he know that God loves him and will never stop caring for him.

> *There are some things we can only learn when we're still and God has our undivided attention.*

David was missing the point of his anointing and God's favor, so he needed to have his life shaken up a little to remember his purpose. God allowed a night season in his life to say, "Hold up, David. You're getting it twisted. You're not anointed because you're David; you're anointed because I'm protecting you, and *I say* that you're anointed. None of this is about you. The only reason your enemies haven't won is because *I've* been defeating them. You have no idea how much I've been protecting you. Don't get arrogant and make me remove Myself from these situations."

David was upset when God suddenly felt absent. He didn't understand why he had to retreat from battles and pray for protection instead of claiming victory. That said, when David's life went into a tailspin, he responded in the correct way—by recognizing his error in thinking he had his life under control and by turning to his Creator. David said, "Lord, I'm sorry. I won't get it twisted again. I will give You all the glory and praise." David called upon the Lord in his night season, and God restored him.

Take Time to Listen and Learn

There are some things we can only hear when everything is silent, and there are some things we can only learn when we're still and God has our undivided attention. Growth doesn't happen in the battle but when God calls you to take a step back from your situation.

I enjoy working out, and I've learned a few things about muscles at the gym. One is that muscles don't grow while you're working out; they grow when you rest in recovery. Sure, they swell when you're pumping iron, but that's not growth. When you drink some protein, lie down and rest, you build up strength.

Nights come to mature us—to deepen our devotion to the Lord through a period that isn't about doing but about listening and obeying. It's in the stillness that you can hear God say, "Now that you're here, let Me teach you something." Being forced to rest can be frustrating, but it's good to get to the point where the only thing you know to do is pray and cry out to the Lord.

Don't Get Lost in the Dark

A new day doesn't start when the sun comes up. It's at midnight, the darkest part of the night, when day begins. Similarly it's only when you're willing to completely empty yourself, rest in stillness and accept God's work in your life that you'll be able to experience your dawn.

Now when the morning comes, God expects you to be different as a result of the night. You can't keep doing what you were doing before the night came. When a night ends, it leads into a new day; consequently, when a night season comes, it's time for a new season in your life.

Nights are meant to challenge us and draw us to something greater. If morning comes around and you're still doing what you used to do, you can expect another night season. I'm reminded of the movie *Groundhog Day* in which Bill Murray's character keeps waking up at 6 a.m. to live the same day all over again because he continually fails to learn his lesson. Have you ever felt like you were struggling with the same thing over and over instead of allowing yourself to grow? You'll keep experiencing the same painful period—until you learn your lesson! When God teaches us something new in our nights, we need to grow.

Night seasons call us to a new way of being, which means we also have to adopt a new God-centered way of thinking. This means we should test everything in our lives to see if the things of our yesterdays fit into our tomorrows. We need to let go of whatever does not line up with God's agenda.

If someone comes between God and me, I'm going to choose God every time. I know it doesn't work when I try to control my life, so I'm willing to turn it over to the Lord, because He'll work it out for my best.

When God is at work in your life, you should tell your friends, "I am getting new. I'm not going to cry all night and be the same thing I was before this started. I'm not going to struggle all night and then, when joy comes, act the same way as before the weeping. God has initiated a night season in my life, so I'm going to accept His instruction in anticipation of something new and better."

Are you ready for renewal? Then hold onto the promise that joy is coming.

Dawn Is Coming!

There's one more thing I love about Psalm 30. It teaches us that night seasons have a limit. It may sound simple and sophomoric, but nights have beginnings, and they have endings. Thank God that joy comes in the morning! I know the morning is coming because God promises that troubles won't last forever—*this too shall pass*.

Joy is coming.

Since you know that joy is coming, you can start acting on that faith now. Even if you're crying on the inside, you can claim joy. Even if you're in the midst of it, you can act like you have victory. Even if you feel like you're losing it, you can know it's going to be all right because you can trust the Word more than you can trust your circumstances.

You see, we walk by faith and not by sight. Since God has your back, you can trust that joy will come in the morning. You can believe that weeping will only last for a night season, and joy will be born out of your heartache. After all your tears and problems, you'll wake up one morning refreshed and rejuvenated.

I can't tell you when your night season is going to end, but I can tell you that it has a time limit. It won't last forever. One thing is certain: you have lessons to learn from your night season, and God is history's *greatest* teacher.

Discussion Questions

1. Read Ecclesiastes 3, which starts out with the verse "To every thing there is a season, and a time to every purpose under the heaven." What season are you currently going through? What might God be trying to teach you?

2. In your time of distress, can you say, "I waited patiently for the LORD; and he inclined unto me, and heard my cry" (Ps. 40:1)? When was the last time you were quiet before the Lord? How can you find time to peacefully wait in silence for Him to speak?

3. Have you ever gotten arrogant over your blessings and abilities? What was the result? Read James 1:17. How does understanding that every gift you possess comes from the Lord alter your self-perception?

4. Are you stuck repeating the same night season? Do you keep dealing with the same problems? Christ has set us free from our sins. How can you, through Him, find victory in your situation?

Action Point: Make a list of the things that seem wrong in your life. Then search the Bible for God's promises in those areas and pray, claiming those truths over your life.

8

IT'S TIME TO CHANGE

And when he came to himself, he said, How many hired servants of my father's have bread enough and to spare, and I perish with hunger! I will arise and go to my father, and will say unto him, Father, I have sinned against heaven, and before thee, And am no more worthy to be called thy son: make me as one of thy hired servants. And he arose, and came to his father.   Luke 15:17–20

We need to trust God at all times, but let's be honest— it's not easy when we're stuck in a dark stillness. We tend to hunker down and wait for the situation to blow over instead of opening ourselves to transformation. In order to reap the benefit of a night season, however, we have to accept the change our new day brings.

"Change" is a two-way street. God may have a work to do in your life, but you're not going to reach your full potential unless you give up your control and accept His leading. When God pulls you into a "night," you don't just have to suffer through. Instead, you need to accept your situation, listen to the Lord, grow in your dependence on Him, and emerge into the new "day" as a transformed creature.

While you may be excited for your new season, change can be intimidating. We want our lives to be steady and consistent. Fear of the unknown can cause us to get stuck in our problems. We often have the same night season, not because we can't but because we *won't* change.

Have you ever fought a change, even though you knew that its eventual outcome would be positive? Have you ever avoided doing something new because you didn't want to let go of what was familiar? Remember Chris Rock's character Pookie in the film *New Jack City*? Referring to his crack addiction, he says, "It just keeps calling me." He can't escape because he keeps returning to what he has always known—even though it's slowly destroying him. Do you feel like Pookie—having to answer your issue every time it calls? Well, it's time to disconnect the phone. It's time to turn the drama in your life over to God and allow Him to work so His is the only call you answer.

The truth is that we're all broken. We all need to be fixed.

It's Time to Move On

Do you feel like you've lost control? Do you find yourself so focused on a problem you're unable to function? Accepting that you're lost without God's help is the first step to correcting your mess. That said, admitting that something is going wrong in your life is challenging.

We are, by nature, creatures who like to have it all together. Admitting something is wrong is challenging, so we try to operate as if our lives were picture perfect. The truth is, however, that we're all broken. We all need to be fixed. We all need to experience the Lord's transforming power, and in order to do this, we have to be open to change.

In fact, the first question you need to ask yourself is do I even *want* to change? You see, changing means leaving a known hell to go to an unknown heaven, and many of us would rather wallow in our comfortable, familiar "hell" than open ourselves to God's challenging, yet ultimately good, reformation. If we're honest, many of us avoid letting go of the drama in our lives until it gets so bad that we're *forced* to change.

The problem is that you can't just snap your fingers, change and be done with it. It takes serious effort to transform your habits.

If you know anything about twelve-step programs, you know that a preparatory step always comes before the action steps. You have to take a fearless moral inventory and reevaluate your purpose. You have to look straight at your problem, accept it and fix it.

I know what you're thinking: "Whatever. This message isn't for me. I'm not even dealing with any major problems!" Remember that not all problems *look* messy. It might seem like everything is going well for you, yet you might be struggling in your relationship with God. You may be prosperous in your finances and relationships and doing "good things"—yet acting outside God's will. So what do you do? Confess that you're an undeserving sinner and no better than anyone else. Humbling yourself is the first step to receiving God's forgiveness and grace.

Stop Settling

I love the story of the Prodigal Son from Luke 15. You've probably heard it before, but it has some fresh things to teach you about dealing with transformation.

The story starts when the younger son of a family—let's call him Sam—approaches his father one day and says, "Daddy, give me my inheritance." In asking for his portion of the family's property, Sam uses the Greek term *bios*, which roughly means he asked for the things (wealth, goods, resources etc.) by which life is sustained. You see, Sam's perspective was warped from the beginning because he thought living was defined by having stuff.

Anyway, Sam asks for the part of the estate entitled to him, which, since he's the youngest, averages out to about one third of his father's assets. Jewish sons typically waited for their fathers to die to claim their inheritance; Sam is a good Jewish boy, so he knows what he's asking is wrong. At this point in the story, however, he's more interested in money than morality. He's able to justify his actions by focusing on material gain, so he has no desire or motivation to change.

> *Instead of returning home to confess his mistakes, the son willingly became a slave.*

After gathering up his possessions, Sam leaves home and, as the Bible says, begins living riotously. During this period of his life, he squanders away the entirety of his inheritance. This is where things get sticky. Sam runs out of money and into problems.

Luke says that after the youngest son had spent everything, there was a great famine in the land, and Sam hired himself out to a man to work in his pigpen. Instead of returning home to confess his mistakes, the son willingly became a slave. We often think of the sty as the unfortunate location where he gets stuck, but when you look at the text, it states that he *chose to go there*. Rather than seeking help, he attempted to help himself.

Like Sam, we like to live our own way, even if that sometimes means disregarding what we know is right. We'd rather be slaves in a distant land like Sam than return "home" and accept God's leading. We do our best to ignore our struggles and to remain in control of our lives—plowing forward instead of turning to God. While we might be able to manage a self-centered lifestyle for a while, that kind of living will eventually catch up with us.

Look at Sam. Living in a riotous way involves tension and tragedy, so ending up in the pigsty probably wasn't his first bump with drama. Multiple negative decisions—combined with his aversion to returning home—led him to the pigs.

Being with the pigs did finally get to Sam, and verse 17 says that he came to his senses and realized he needed to return home.

We too should realize our need to be in our Father's presence. I once read about a man who burst into a church demanding to see Howard. "Howard?" the deacons asked. "Who in the world is Howard?" The man said, "I don't know. All I know is that he's supposed to be here. I've been out in the world too long, you see, and I need to talk to him." The deacons exchanged confused glances until the man continued, "When I was little, Momma used to bring me to this church, and whenever the congregation prayed, they'd say, 'Our Father, who art in Heaven, Howard be Thy name. . . .'"

Like the Prodigal Son, everyone needs to maintain relationship with the Father in order to be transformed. "Living in the far country" like the son means knowingly being out of the will of God. If you've been living with the pigs, get fed up and run to the Lord. Go home.

Deal with What's Real

When the son realizes he's worse off than his father's slaves, he goes *home* to repair his relationship with his dad. Instead of trying to figure out a way to get out of the pigpen while remaining in the far country, he decides to come clean and tell his father he sinned against him.

It's a simple message, but it's also powerful—the son doesn't try to make excuses; he deals with the heart of the issue and says to his father, "I have sinned against heaven, and I have sinned against thee." The Prodigal Son reveals his willingness to revamp his life when he remembers the person to whom he truly owes his confession.

Can you go to your Father and admit your failings?

Before healing can occur, you need to confess your deep-rooted issues. The son admits that what he did was ultimately against his father. Can you, like him, go to your Father and admit your failings?

Instead of resolving our deep issues, we prefer to try to manage our messes. Real change, however, is ontological and not peripheral. That's a fancy way of saying we have to deal with our real problems instead of always focusing on side issues.

In order to be transformed in Christ, you have to find the root of your spiritual problem—you have to recognize that you're in a pigpen and that you need a life overhaul.

You can't expect to understand God's plans for your life if you refuse to ask Him and listen to His commands. I've found that when I maintain a disciplined devotional life— reading the Word, praying daily and staying in strong fellowship and right relationship with God—and when I'm focused on the Lord's will for my life, I'm able to see a major pitfall ten miles down the road.

You don't need to impress anyone when you're alone with God.

When I let my prayer and study life fall by the wayside, I quickly find myself running on fumes in my spiritual life. When my faith is faulty, I'm always surprised by problems and blame them on everything other than my relationship with God.

Listen, you don't need to try to impress anyone when you're alone with God. Focus on resolving the real, deep issues and getting back into the Lord's home. Tell Him what's going on and ask for His help, and the rest will eventually fall into place.

Sam missed the message for a long time. While he was living recklessly and had stuff, he had all kinds of folk, but when the stuff ran out, so did his "friends." When famine hit his country, he found himself moneyless and friendless. Thankfully, Sam recognized that the issue was not that he had run out of money or people. The issue was that he was not in his father's house.

Nowadays many people run to the church for cash and camaraderie, treating Jesus like a "Get Out of the Pigpen Free" card. But this isn't the way it works. God cares about our hearts—not our earthly goods and accomplishments. In order to receive His blessings, we have to humble ourselves and return to His presence.

Listen, I don't know what you're wrestling with or what changes you might need to make, but I know you need to get back to the Father's house. Deal with your personal spiritual setbacks and get back to a right relationship with God.

God Restores Repentant Spirits

When the son recognizes his mistake, goes home and confesses the error of his ways, he is blessed beyond what he deserves. You see, in many ways the pigpen is a symbol of grace. It provides the environment in which Sam recognizes his need to be restored to his father.

When we stray away, God longs for our return.

Okay, so Sam has a change of heart in the sty, and he heads home. When he gets close enough to the house, his father—who apparently had been watching for his return—runs to embrace his son.

God treats His children in a similar fashion. He loves us unconditionally and longs to live in close communion with us. When we stray away, He longs for our return. Even if we get beat up and smelly from living in our own pigpens for too long, God will rush to greet us when we make the effort to get back into His presence.

The road back to a strong relationship with God might not be easy, but don't give up. Look at Sam. When he makes a decision to return home, he follows through with it and is welcomed by his loving father.

But the story isn't over yet. The father doesn't just welcome Sam home and send him out to work the fields. Instead, when Sam returns home, the father tells his servants to place a signet ring on his son's finger that signifies that he's an authority in the home, shoes on his feet to show that he's not a slave, and robes around his shoulders to reveal that he's covered and protected by his father.

While he was in the far country, the son couldn't enjoy the benefits of being his father's child—but he was always loved. By picking himself up and hauling himself home, he was able to reclaim the symbols of his sonship.

If you're willing to change whatever is holding you back from God, you can claim Christ's power, freedom and provision in your life. The Bible says that the Lord has the power to restore the years that the canker worm has eaten. In other words, He can take away the bitterness of your past and make you whole again in Him.

God loves you regardless of your state of obedience or disobedience. He'll never abandon you, but He can't bless you when you're living in the far country. If you return to the Father's house, however, you will be restored to a right relationship with God and can reclaim your joy, your security and your peace.

Don't Get Discouraged!

Unfortunately, sometimes your problem isn't just between you and God. Sometimes other people try to mess up your progress. When you change to get right with God, some folk might not be willing to rejoice alongside you.

This happens to Sam. Verse 25 says that when the younger son returns home, his older brother hears the celebration. The estate must have had a serious party going on. They were really celebrating Sam's return. I mean, they weren't waltz-ing; they were *getting it in.* Knowing the meaning of the music and dancing, the older brother was less than pleased.

> *If others don't like what God is doing in your life, their issue is with Him, not with you.*

The older brother—who had responsibly refrained from wasting his inheri-tance—didn't appreciate the fuss everyone was making over Sam, so he did two things. First, he refused to go to the party. He didn't want to support or to congratulate his little bro's progress in humbling himself and returning home. Sec-ond, he gossiped, recalling Sam's years of reckless living and being out in the world.

Jealous of the extravagance with which his younger brother was received, the older brother accused his father of being unfair. He said, "Daddy, I have been with you all this time, and you never sacrificed a fattened calf for me and my friends."

The older brother didn't like the way the situation was handled, so he voiced his objections to Sam's reacceptance. Notably, the older brother didn't air his grievances to Sam; he took his complaints to his father.

This tells me something: if others don't like what God is doing in your life, their issue is with Him, not with you. If others don't like that you've regained your peace and joy, their issue is with God.

Sam's brother whined that his treatment was unfair. But, you see, God isn't "fair," and we should be thankful for this fact. No, the younger son didn't *deserve* to be welcomed home in such a way, but aren't you glad he was? Aren't you glad he was shown grace and mercy beyond what he had earned?

You, like Sam, can say, "I have been in the far country, and I don't deserve this party. But Daddy gave me a party, so I am going to celebrate. I was down and out, but he brought me up and in." Don't let yourself be distracted by others' negative comments. Your faith has nothing to do with others' perspectives and everything to do with trusting the Lord for your own journey.

If you're tired of where you are right now, you should declare a day of independence. Assert that you are no longer dependent on your old problems, your old sin, your old friends and your old self. Don't allow yourself to continue to be controlled by issues of the past. Because God is greater than anything this world can throw at you, He can give you victory over everything holding you back from who you're meant to be. It's time to sing like R&B artist Jennifer Hudson, "I am changing, trying every way that I can. I am changing."

Are you ready to take that next step toward change? You need to move forward in Jesus' name. It's time to return to your Father's house. If you're in the far country, you need to *change* your address.

Discussion Questions:

1. Read the "Parable of the Lost Sheep" and the "Parable of the Lost Coin" in Luke 15:1-10. How do these stories relate to the story of the Prodigal Son? What do they reveal about the Lord's character?

2. What is something that seems to control your life? What steps can you take to stop answering your problem every time it calls? Who might you be able to share this burden with?

3. How are you like the Prodigal Son? What might tempt you to "live in the far country" (success in the world's eyes, sensual pleasures, etc.), and how can you overcome those desires? What areas of your life do you need to turn back over to the Father's control?

4. Have you ever had a problem turn into a blessing because it opened your eyes to something greater? How can you change your perspective to praise God for *everything* in your life?

Action Point: The Bible says that "all have sinned, and come short of the glory of God" (Rom. 3:23). Are you willing to admit that you're a sinner? How have you sinned against the Holy Father? Ask the Lord for His forgiveness, because His grace covers *all* sins.

9

I GOT THIS

And when the servant of the man of God was risen early, and gone forth, behold, an host compassed the city both with horses and chariots. And his servant said unto him, Alas, my master! how shall we do? And he answered, Fear not: for they that be with us are more than they that be with them. And Elisha prayed, and said, LORD, I pray thee, open his eyes, that he may see. And the LORD opened the eyes of the young man; and he saw: and, behold, the mountain was full of horses and chariots of fire round about Elisha.   2 Kings 6:15–17

We've been learning how God often uses struggles to draw us closer to Him, but this is only half the story. Sometimes you're living correctly yet facing a trying time the Lord didn't initiate. So what do you do when you're positive you're following the Lord's will yet dealing with a lot of dirt? How do you handle a real spiritual attack?

The first step to resisting spiritual attacks is firming up your relationship with Christ. When you're living right with God, you'll still face storms, but you'll be able to weather them through His power.

We shouldn't get discouraged when we face opposition. Yes, the devil is relentless in his desire to see us fall, but Christ tells us, "Blessed are ye, when men shall revile you, and persecute you, and shall say all manner of evil against you falsely, for my sake. Rejoice, and be exceeding glad: for great is your reward in heaven" (Matt. 5:11–12).

It goes against all of our earthly understanding to say, "Hallelujah, I'm blessed!" when we're struggling—yet that's what we're called to do. So how do we maintain the right perspective and remember God's omnipotence when the devil is giving us grief? Only by understanding our spiritual resources can we see our problems through God's lens and prevent Satan's attacks from hurting our minds and wrecking our lives.

> *Satan does not come directly to kill but rather to lead astray.*

Satan, the Great Deceiver

Satan's influence is sometimes difficult to identify in a situation, because he comes to us as a deceiver. When you see Satan in Scripture, he does not come *directly* to kill but rather to lead astray. Let's check the record.

In the Garden of Eden, Satan didn't force Adam or Eve to disobey—he simply misinformed and distracted them from their purpose: "Why don't you eat that yummy-looking fruit? You won't die—in fact, it will make you smart! God just doesn't want to share His knowledge. Go on, eat it." Adam and Eve then made their own decision.

After the Holy Spirit led Jesus to wander in the desert for forty days, Satan came to tempt Him: "Are you *really* the Son of God? Then prove it." Satan threw everything he had into tricking Christ to sin. He played at Christ's physical hunger, His authority and His divine protection. Since

Satan didn't have the ability to overturn Christ's power, he took a more subtle, yet equally dangerous, approach—deception.

When Jesus told His disciples He had to go to Jerusalem to suffer, be killed, placed in the grave and rise again on the third day, Satan pushed Peter to say, "Don't do that! Why go to Jerusalem?" Now, Jesus knew that He had a purpose to fulfill, so He wasn't

Satan loves nothing more than getting you alone and tricking you into giving up.

about to take the easy way out. That said, we do know from Christ's agonizing struggle in the Garden of Gethsemane that He felt Satan's temptations. Still He never lost sight of His responsibility, so He knew Peter's words were ungodly. He responded, "Get thee behind me, Satan: thou art an offence unto me: for thou savourest not the things that be of God, but those that be of men" (Matt. 16:23). You see Satan doesn't conquer by brute force—he tries to *deceive* us with worldly comforts and pleasures that pale in comparison to God's greater plan.

So what does it mean for your life that Satan is a deceiver? Well, have you ever tried to sort through some upsetting situation and had Satan come along to suggest that you're the only one this certain thing ever happened to, that no one cares about you, and that you're stuck and are never going to escape? Satan is a *liar,* and he knows how to poke us where it hurts. He's talented at provoking us to anger, hurt—or worst of all, despair. Satan loves nothing more than getting you alone and tricking you into giving up.

Listen: you don't have to buy into the Adversary's lies.

Jesus already won your battle by defeating the devil. You might have to struggle with serious temptations, but through Christ, you can claim victory. Don't give in to Satan's deceptions!

Use Your Gifting

Let's be honest: a real attack of the devil is scary. Satan wants to discourage us on a far more serious level than the minor problems we tend to blame on him—like spilling a cup of coffee on a white shirt or getting stuck in traffic. And when you're in the middle of an attack, it can be pretty disconcerting.

So how do you handle a spiritual attack? Let's look at the example of Elisha in Second Kings chapter 6 where he and his servant find themselves literally surrounded by the enemy.

If you read back a little bit before our verse, you learn that the king of Syria was planning an attack on Israel, but Elisha kept foiling the Syrian king's plans by telling Israel's king what was being plotted. The Syrian king finally realized that unless he got rid of Elisha, he was never going to bring down his enemy. So instead of launching an attack against Israel, he sent his army after Elisha—a man who was simply using his gift to do God's work.

Now before you decide you're just like Elisha, favored by the Lord and only being attacked by Satan because you're a great Christian, take some time for a little self-examination. Sometimes you struggle not because Satan is pushing you off the right path but because you weren't on the right path in the first place. Christ doesn't want to see you acting holy and refusing to admit your own problems.

But if you're not in the wrong, and you're still experiencing difficulties, it might be because the devil has decided he needs to keep you from using your gifts. Maybe your gifts are frustrating Satan because they're keeping him from fulfilling his agendas to pull apart relationships and to tear apart your life.

Why would Satan want to attack when you were closely walking with God? Let me explain with an illustration from basketball. Do you remember Eric Snow, a retired point guard for the Cleveland Cavaliers? While I really liked Snow, he couldn't shoot a ball to save his life. He played alongside LeBron James, and it was hysterical to watch the way the defense would line up when they were on the court. If Snow had the ball, he would be left almost entirely open, even at the top of the key. When LeBron had the ball, however, he'd have three guys on him. The defense knew that LeBron had a gift for making hoops, so they did everything in their power to stop him. They weren't too worried about Eric on offense, so they let him take his shots.

> *Only when your abilities line up with God's will do things really happen.*

If God has not given you a specific gift or directed you to a place, you aren't going to face much opposition. Only when your abilities line up with God's will do things really happen. So when God gives you a purpose and the skill to fulfill it, that's when the devil is going to try to thwart your progress. He doesn't want you to make it down the court and score one for the Kingdom.

A little background helps us understand what's happening

here. Before Lucifer's fall, he was up in heaven, coveting God's position. He tried to deceive other angels into joining his cause to take what belonged to God, but he failed and was cast into hell. Even now that he's only the lowly prince of the earth, Satan still wants God's stuff. That's why you're under attack. When Satan comes after you, he's coming after God in you. If you weren't doing anything for the Kingdom, you wouldn't be a threat, and he would say, just like he says to everyone else, "Go ahead and take your best shot."

Satan doesn't want you to be a blessing to your family, your co-workers or your community. Because he's afraid of what you're doing in God's name, Satan attacks when you use your gifting. For this reason you can rejoice in your suffering. When others harass you when you're following God, you know that you have a faith of value.

> *Many of us fail to maintain spiritual hope because we get stuck focusing on our natural struggles.*

God loves you so much that He put treasure in you in the form of your gift. You are a child of God, and as such, you have something to offer. Don't let Satan keep you from that purpose.

Open Your Eyes!

Let's get back to Elisha, because he has some things to teach us about spiritual attacks. War horses and chariots surround him, but he remains calm. Naturally speaking, the odds were against him and his servant. But when the servant cries out, "Ahh! Just *look* at all those chariots! What are we going to do?!" Elisha, seeing the situation spiritually, responds, "Chill out. Why are you so worried? There are more for us than against us."

Many of us fail to maintain spiritual hope because we get stuck focusing on our natural struggles. In the physical realm it's always going to seem like you don't have enough money and your family is going to fall apart and you're going to lose your job. But listen to what Elisha says, "You're not looking at this thing right."

You have to see your problems from God's perspective. Why? First, anything you're dealing with will pale in comparison to the Lord's power. Second, you'll see that you have a lot more going for you than you realize.

My grandma used to sing, "All day, all night, there are angels watching over me, Lord." There are some spiritual warriors ready to fight on your behalf. They have your back and your front. They're walking beside you—protecting you from danger seen and unseen. Even though you might see problems heading your way, you have heavenly powers you can't even see working for your good.

Don't assume you're outnumbered when you're only staring at the natural. The Bible says, "For though we walk in the flesh, we do not war after the flesh: (For the weapons of our warfare are not carnal, but mighty through God to the pulling down of strong holds)" (2 Cor. 10:3–4). You don't need to fear physical battles, because you are spiritually empowered. Angels are waiting to help you out.

Therefore you can say, "I might be attacked in the natural, but I'm not going to fight in the natural, because that is not how I've been equipped. Cussing you out is not my weapon. Giving you attitude is not my weapon. I don't fight dirt with dirt, because *my weapons are in the spiritual realm.*

You don't want me to get on my hands and knees in prayer, because that's when the angels show up."

I know for a fact that God watches out for His children's spiritual well-being. My enemies may have surrounded me, but they have fallen one by one—not thanks to me but to the God I serve.

Believe for Yourself

Here's the problem: I can preach at you until I'm blue in the face, but it isn't going to make a difference in your life until you personally experience the Lord's freeing power. I can give you verse after verse, but until *you* learn it and believe it, you're going to be on a spiritual rollercoaster—going to church or reading a devotional when you want to feel happy or inspired and then returning to living low. You have to claim faith and hope for yourself.

> *You have to see for yourself that there are more for you than against you.*

Elisha understood this. No matter how many times he told his servant it was all right, nothing would change until the young man saw it for himself. Despite Elisha's assertion that they had more on their side than against them, the young man apparently continued to worry. So Elisha prayed that God would make his servant see the truth: "Lord, open his eyes. *I know* that You're with us and that You're going to bring us through, but just telling him isn't fixing his fear. Open his eyes so he can see the reality of what's happening."

The Lord answered, and the young man's eyes were opened, and he saw all the chariots of fire lined up to fight for them. Then he knew for himself that it would work out.

You see, it's not enough for someone else to know that you're going to be all right—*you* have to know it. The preacher can't come to your house every time your enemies show up. He can't make you see it like he sees it. You have to be able to see for yourself that there are more for you than against you.

When the devil attacks you, look him dead in the eye and say, "Because of the promises of God, I got this. I have people praying for me, and I have angels on my right and angels on my left. No matter how hard it gets, I'm going to make it."

Even if your enemies are surrounding you and everything feels wrong, God will protect and sustain you. If you need money, He'll supply according to His riches in glory. If you need love, He'll provide it in deep abundance. If you need peace of mind, He'll give you a calm that passes understanding.

If you feel the devil working to counteract the goodness of God in your life, tell him he can't have your joy and your peace. Tell him you're going to keep using your gifts for God's kingdom. He can't do anything to stop it, because you have a serious support system lined up.

Now is the time to believe *for yourself* that God has your back. You got this.

Discussion Questions:

1. "Put on the whole armour of God, that ye may be able to stand against the wiles of the devil. For we wrestle not against flesh and blood, but against principalities,

against powers, against the rulers of the darkness of this world, against spiritual wickedness in high places" (Eph. 6:11–12). Do you believe that demonic forces are real and at work in this world? How can you prepare your heart and mind to defend yourself against Satan's deceptions? (Hint: check out Ephesians 6:14–18 where the specifics of God's armor are discussed.)

2. What lies does Satan tell you (e.g. "You're not X enough to do Y")? Which of God's truths (e.g. "I am fearfully and wonderfully made" Ps. 139:14) can you claim so you can have victory over those deceptions?

3. Are you under spiritual attack? What indicators suggest that your struggles are spiritual rather than normal physical battles? How can you trust God to bring you through?

4. Have you ever known someone who was fixated on a limited problem when you saw a clear answer? What did you do to help that person see the bigger picture? How might you apply those same tactics to your own crises? How does knowing that God holds *the truth* to every situation alter your personal perspective?

Action point: Take some time to pray over the spiritual obstacles in your life. Claim God's supernatural power over your natural struggles. Wait on God to speak His truth into your life and to proclaim His power over your situation.

10

AIN'T GONNA LET NOBODY TURN ME AROUND

Thou therefore, my son, be strong in the grace that is in Christ Jesus. And the things that thou hast heard of me among many witnesses, the same commit thou to faithful men, who shall be able to teach others also. Thou therefore endure hardness, as a good soldier of Jesus Christ. No man that warreth entangleth himself with the affairs of this life; that he may please him who hath chosen him to be a soldier. And if a man also strive for masteries, yet is he not crowned, except he strive lawfully. 2 Timothy 2:1–5

I have news for you: life is hard. "Enduring hardness" is not, however, something those of us in Western society often like to do. Our culture tells us to buy products to make our lives easier and to view relationships as worthwhile only when they're romantically simple. But this mentality totally misses the mark!

My ancestors knew how to keep fighting no matter what their circumstances. Trapped behind the confining bars of slavery, they learned how to sing the sweet song of the caged bird. Caged birds sing even more beautifully than free birds, because their songs are tempered and refined by their difficulties. Their song of freedom is movingly real, because they know what it costs and the hardness that has to be endured to obtain it. Like caged birds, we should learn to function within our circumstances while trusting and hoping that a brighter day will come.

When situations get sticky, you can't just give up. When you face obstacles, you can't just turn around. There's an old spiritual that goes:

> Ain't gonna let nobody turn me around.
> Ain't gonna let segregation turn me around.
> Ain't gonna let hatred turn me around.
> Ain't gonna let no Jim Crow turn me around.
> Keep on a-singing, keep on a-swinging.
> Gonna build a brand new world.

Don't give up right before a breakthrough! Don't let anything distract you from your purpose. Keep going!

You Can't Do It Alone

The first step to having a strong Christian walk involves understanding you can't make it alone. You'll never get anywhere if you insist on pridefully laboring to succeed alone. Making a positive impact involves having a like-minded community to support you.

Reread the verse at the beginning of this chapter. Paul started the church in Ephesus and stayed there about eighteen months. Then, in typical apostolic fashion, he went to continue his work of starting up churches and training ministerial leaders, leaving Timothy, one of his spiritual protégées, in charge at Ephesus.

In Paul's first letter to Timothy, he gave basic instructions on how to ordain elders and deacons in the church.

In his second, Paul backs up what he discussed in the first. While Timothy drew his strength from Christ, he also benefited from having a strong mentor. Paul reminds Timothy that he can't make it on his own strength: "Thou therefore, my son, be strong in the grace that is in Christ Jesus" (2 Tim. 2:5).

> *In order for you to finish and finish well, you need people to encourage you in your purpose and to challenge you to stay close to God.*

In order for you to finish and finish well, you need people to encourage you in your purpose and to challenge you to stay close to God. Only by strengthening yourself through Christian fellowship can you grow in your God-given purpose. What call do you feel God has placed on your life, and how can you answer it with the help of other godly men and women?

Do Your Duty

The gist of Paul's letter is to encourage Timothy to do his duty and to do it well. Unfortunately, duty has gotten a bad rap in this generation. We tend to only want to do what is convenient and what we feel like doing. When we're on the Lord's team, however, we can't just do whatever seems enjoyable at the moment; we have to do the duties we've been called to perform.

Duties aren't optional. Some stuff can't just be put down or thrown away when you decide you don't want to deal with it anymore. You have to take responsibility.

Now that's not to say we can't enjoy our tasks. It's my

duty to be a faithful husband to my wife, but I love her, so it's also my passion. It's my duty to raise my kids, but I want them to grow up correctly, so it's also my passion. It's my duty to be a pastor, but I care deeply about Enon's congregation, so it's also my passion.

Duty can be overwhelming, but one of the many great things about God is that He calls each of us to fulfill a specific purpose. He'll never ask you to do more than what you're able. Even if your calling seems big in your eyes, God has it under control.

God calls each of us to fulfill a specific purpose.

Let's take Timothy's duty for example. His duty was basically to lead everyone to Christ. How overwhelming! But Timothy knew that to have a strong witness, he had to be significant in others' lives, and he accepted the challenge. His duty was not just to live quietly as a good Timothy; it was to give to others what Paul had given to him: "The things that thou hast heard of me among many witnesses, the same commit thou to faithful men, who shall be able to teach others also" (2 Tim. 2:2). Like Timothy you need to reach out to those around you to teach them about God's goodness. The Lord will show you how, but you need to listen to His Word and do what He asks.

You need to be faithful where you are instead of sitting around waiting for God to bring along something new. You have to be faithful in the here and now. The grass isn't greener on the other side of the fence—that's just false advertising. The truth of the matter is that you have to work hard—planting and watering your own grass; then you'll find you have a lush lawn right where you are with no need to climb over the fence for Astroturf.

No one can do your duty for you, so find your purpose in Christ, and live it!

Why Is This So Hard?!

Here's where this whole purpose thing gets sticky: doing your duty is often difficult. Paul tells Timothy to "endure hardness." You need to remember that even if God has given you a purpose and a duty, you will face hardships.

When I think of enduring hardness, I think of having to walk to school as a kid. Today the buses run everywhere, but I had to trudge through three feet of snow in the winter. Mom would rub Vaseline on my face, and off I would go. The wind would blow, but I'd keep walking—even when my face got red and I started looking like Joe Frazier in the eighth round against Muhammad Ali. I kept pushing onward, because turning around was not an option.

Do you know what that feels like—to just keep moving forward? Even if your journey gets difficult and you feel like you're fighting the elements alone, just keep walking.

God will allow difficulties in your life to test whether or not you're really living the way you say you want to live. Trials are going to break you down to your core, so He can rebuild you.

You have to keep asserting that God is good—even when life refuses to cut you any breaks.

Don't Get Distracted

Never allow yourself to take the easy way out when you're struggling to endure hardness. You see the devil doesn't have to win in order to win. All he has to do to claim victory is distract you from your purpose. If he can get you to focus on anything other than God's plans, he has already won.

Second Timothy says, "No man that warreth entangleth himself with the affairs of this life; that he may please him who hath chosen him to be a soldier" (2:4). You can't live with the intention of gaining the world's approval if you want to please your King. Instead of chasing after what this world can offer, dedicate to whole-heartedly serving the Creator of the universe, trusting His purpose and His purpose alone for your life. Like the soldiers at the Tomb of the Unknown Soldier at Arlington or those at Buckingham Palace in London, you have to remain stolidly focused on your duty. Don't allow distractions to steer you away from God's plans.

> *Instead of chasing after what this world can offer, dedicate to whole-heartedly serving the Creator of the universe, trusting His purpose and His purpose alone for your life.*

Timothy never lost sight of his purpose. He knew that he didn't need to please anyone other than Christ, and he lived for that mission. Rather than trying to better himself and prosper in his own life, he accepted God's challenge to turn everyone around him into Timothys. By refusing the temptation to remain silent and blend into the world around him, Timothy stood up and made a strong impact for God's kingdom.

Don't let anyone or anything distract you from what God wants to do in your life. You're meant to soar like an eagle, so don't hang around pigeons. You're meant to be a king or a queen, so stop acting like a joker. You have a purpose in Christ, and you have to assert, "ain't gonna let nobody turn me around."

Winning Right

Once you've heard God's call and accepted your duty, you have to pay attention to *how* you go about living out your purpose. You can't "win" by the world's standards and expect that to be the same as "winning" according to the Lord's will.

Winning is only winning if it honors God.

Way back when I was in college, I tried to get into a fraternity. One of the guys who was already in the organization wanted to test my mettle, so he approached me with two bottles of MD 20/20 and challenged me to a chugging contest.

I wanted to prove myself to him, so I started guzzling the stuff. I got three quarters of the way down the bottle before I realized he had stopped drinking and walked inside. I'd thought I was winning, but instead I was being played. I wasn't victorious—I was just drunk. You probably think I'm crazy for even telling this story, but the point is that if we go about trying to "win" from the world's perspective, we're always going to end up losing. Winning is only winning if it honors God.

"If a man also strive for masteries, yet is he not crowned, except he strive lawfully" (2 Tim. 2:5). You see, mastery is only awarded if you earn it the correct way. It's possible to be successful yet not honor God.

If you're in the ministry but are mean and nasty to people,

then your service doesn't honor God. If your business is built on poor ethical practices, then your success doesn't honor God. If you cheat on your spouse, then your relationship doesn't honor God. God's work has to be done in God's honorable way.

Look at Christ. His life showed us what it looks like to trust, obey and win the right way. His struggle certainly wasn't the easiest way to go, but it was *the way* to be a blessing to the whole world. In the Garden of Gethsemane, He prayed, "God, You know I don't really want to do it this way; nevertheless, not My will, but Yours be done." Jesus accepted His duty and died on the cross to give us eternal life. Early Sunday morning, Christ rose from the grave with all power in His hands. He won the right way.

> *God just doesn't want us to run life's race; He wants to mature us so we can finish life's race* well.

If Jesus could die on the cross for you, then you can live for Him. If Jesus could be buried in a grave for you, you can suffer for Him. And since Jesus arose on Sunday morning, you can know that even if you're currently struggling, you're going to rise again.

Our culture says, "I need to get from point A to point B, and I'm not going to deal with anything that gets in my way," but God uses life's difficulties to refine us. The modern church often says, "If there is a struggle associated with my call, then it must not be of God," but when I read the Bible, I don't see any signs of God being a pragmatist. God doesn't just want us to run life's race; He wants to mature us so we can finish life's race *well.*

God might take you to some strange places, and you might end up against some strange obstacles. But if you hold on to God's hand, you'll not only finish the race—you'll win in a way that is pleasing to God. Then when you reach the end of your journey, you'll hear Him say, "Well done, thou good and faithful servant!" (Matt. 25:21).

If life has gotten rough and you're ready to throw in the towel, start saying to yourself, "I ain't gonna let no ob-stacle turn me around. I ain't gonna let no enemies turn me around. I ain't gonna let no-body turn me around."

I don't know what you're struggling with or how many times you've felt like giving up, but listen: you aren't going to let *anything* stop you from living for God. You've shed too many tears and spent too many sleepless nights agonizing over your struggles. You have a duty to fulfill, and you need to be strong in it.

You might be tempted to reason that God never called you. Oh yes He did—life just got hard.

If you leave your battle to your flesh, you're going to fail. When it gets hard, you might be tempted to reason that God never called you. Oh yes He did—life just got hard. You might try to say, "I feel like the Lord is taking me in a new direction." If He is, great, but more than likely, you need to stick out your difficult situation.

Don't put this book down feeling broken and beat up. Commit to living your life strong in the grace of Jesus Christ! You aren't here to just live and die—you have a duty. You're going to live according to your purpose and God's will, enduring trials as necessary. You're going to win right, so don't let anything turn you around.

Discussion Questions:

1. What are some of your "duties"? Are they also your passions? If so, how? How can you take responsibility for your tasks and enjoy doing them?

2. What can you do to share your God-given gifts with others? What spiritual lessons have you learned that you can share with others?

3. Have you ever known a person who won a prize because he/she cheated? How did it make you feel? Have you ever been guilty of deceit or plagiarism, or taking pride in a dishonest accomplishment? What steps can you take to commit your life to honesty first—even before earthly success?

4. What did Christ's life on earth look like? How did He struggle? How did He win? How can we apply His example to our own lives?

Action Point: In this chapter you read part of the old spiritual "Ain't Gonna' Let Nobody Turn Me Around." What is a song that encourages you to keep walking with Christ—no matter what obstacles get thrown in your path? Connect yourself with some good music that reminds you of who God is, and let the messages of those songs permeate your life. (If you're completely lost as to where to look, I might suggest The Enon Tabernacle Mass Choir's *As for Me and My House*.)

11

JUST KEEP DOING THE RIGHT THING

And when much people were gathered together, and were come to him out of every city, he spake by a parable: A sower went out to sow his seed: and as he sowed, some fell by the way side; and it was trodden down, and the fowls of the air devoured it. And some fell upon a rock; and as soon as it was sprung up, it withered away, because it lacked moisture. And some fell among thorns; and the thorns sprang up with it, and choked it. And other fell on good ground, and sprang up, and bare fruit an hundredfold.
Luke 8:4–8

What comes to mind when you hear the words "do the right thing"? Do you picture something like a kid in a store debating stealing a candy bar with an angel on one shoulder and a devil on the other? As adults, it's a little more complicated than that, but there's still that same sense of inner turmoil. Doing the right thing isn't popular. Doing the right thing isn't easy. Still, we're told that if we want to honor God, we have to keep doing the right thing—regardless of circumstance.

I know you're wondering how Luke 8 deals with doing the right thing, so let's take a look at the text. Often when we read this parable, we identify ourselves with the different types of soil, but I think we also need to examine the role of the sower. No matter what, the sower keeps doing what he has been called to do—he sows seeds across several terrains.

Like the sower, Christians are called to continuously give, and being a giver doesn't just mean tithing in church.

> *If you have Jesus' view of humanity, you understand that life is entirely about blessing others with the gospel message.*

Being a giver means believing that because you've been saved, you exist to be a blessing to someone else. You have to give generously of yourself, telling others how God has worked in your life. Your relationship with God will be demonstrated by the way you treat others.

The Bible says, "God commendeth his love toward us, in that, while we were yet sinners, Christ died for us" (Rom. 5:8). Because Christ died for us and God cares for us, we have a responsibility to share that freeing affection. Loving God should lead to a desire to love others.

Just Keep Sowing . . .

One problem in the modern-day church is that people tend to want their own, personalized blessings from Jesus. But we can't, as Christians, be in it for ourselves. We often get stuck thinking of our own desires instead of caring about those around us. When you truly care about humanity, however, you don't want to be blessed all by yourself; you want others to be better off than you. If you have Jesus' view of humanity, you understand that life is entirely about blessing others with the gospel message.

One of Martin Luther King's best-loved hymns says:

> If I can help somebody as I pass along,
> If I can cheer somebody with a word or song,
> If I can show somebody he's traveling wrong,
> Then my living will not be in vain.
>
> If I can do my duty as a Christian ought,
> If I can bring salvation to a world once wrought,
> If I can spread the message as the Master taught,
> Then my living will not be in vain.

What does loving people look like? First off, you have to forgive those who have hurt you. You can't love if your heart is still bitter. In order to truly love and care for others, you have to put their needs first. You have to make blessing those around you to the best of your ability your priority.

Then—and here's the really hard part—you have to

You have to leave the results of your sowing in God's hands.

leave the results of your sowing in God's hands. You have to let difficulties roll off your back. Even if those you're trying to help hassle and hurt you, keep praying for them and loving them. Even if others have been hardened and embittered by life and remain guarded, you have to keep giving. Your responsibility is to keep throwing seeds, and at some point, they'll hit the right place.

Look at the main character of this parable: a man whose job is to sow. The sower simply scatters the seeds—he doesn't worry about whether or not they're going to grow.

Did you catch that? The man isn't responsible for the crop; he's only responsible for the craft. He trusts God for the harvest. He keeps doing the right thing and lets God handle the outcome.

Maturing in the Christian life isn't just about personal growth—it's also about being an evangelical light in a dark world. It's about doing the right thing—persevering and sharing Christ's truth, even when it's difficult.

You might be thinking, "But Alyn, you don't understand. I've been sowing *forever*, and I'm sick of it. I've been nice to people and gotten nothing in return. I've helped people who have turned around and stabbed me in the back." It's not easy, but God doesn't give up on us, so we shouldn't give up on His calling on our lives.

Think about the times Jesus has showered His grace and mercy on you and you've thrown it back in His face. I know I'm guilty of telling the Lord I'll never do a stupid thing again if He'll just fix my problem one time. Then, two weeks later, I find myself back on my knees crying, "God, I truly am sorry! Never again!" I don't like that I do this. I'd rather not admit it. But I'm extremely thankful that God didn't just give up on me. He kept sowing even when my intentions were messed up and my heart was hard. He waited patiently for His seeds of truth and joy to take root.

Following God's example, we need to learn how to keep giving and keep sowing—no matter what our circumstances or conditions that surround us!

In the parable of the sower, only a small portion of the seeds sown grow and thrive, but the sower didn't lose hope for the harvest. Sometimes you might feel like you're never going to see success. But listen: you can't give up on life because one person didn't return your love. You can't stop being nice because one person was mean to you.

If you're feeling jaded, you need to forgive those who have hurt you so you can start sowing again. Don't let memories from the past keep you from doing the Lord's work in your future. Don't wait to turn your disappointments over to Christ. Don't wait to forgive. Don't stop sowing, giving and loving.

One of the things I've learned about myself over the years is that I find personal failure debilitating. I asked myself, "Why does it bother me when what I do isn't immediately and obviously successful?" I had to admit that it was because my life was far too focused on my own performance. I realized that if I

Jesus' parable is designed to explain that He wants His followers to keep sowing despite every setback.

found my identity in my success, I wouldn't know who I was when I messed up. When I found my identity in God, however, no matter what came of my work, I was always somebody in Christ.

Christ calls us to sow, and He'll bless our efforts when they come from a pure heart. Even in our weaknesses, He is strong, so He can magnify every effort. He'll bring our works to fruition in the right place at the right time.

Keep On Keeping On

Let's dig back into Luke 8. Why would Jesus teach this parable at the beginning of the disciples' ministry? He was trying to get His disciples to understand that if they were going to hang out with Him, there were going to be some complications. Following Christ isn't always a party.

Jesus' parable is designed to explain that He wants His

followers to keep sowing despite every setback. It's like He's saying: "I want you guys to sow everywhere we go. But I'm telling you right now that sometimes you're going to sow, and the seeds are going to get thrown right back in your face. You're going to sow, and people are going to mock and even stone you. You're going to sow, and you're going to get talked about and chased away.

"Foxes have holes and birds of the air have nests, but the Son of Man has nowhere to lay His head. You aren't always going to be welcomed with opened arms. If you're scared, back out now. If you always have to have people on your side, back out now. If everyone has to say yes to you all the time, back out now. Because I am about to start a *Star Trek* mission to boldly go where no church has gone before."

> *Some seeds took root and produced a plentiful crop.*

You see, Jesus was preparing His disciples. He wanted them to know that serving Him wasn't going to be easy. All Christ's followers need to keep giving—even when there aren't earthly rewards and successes.

Now we can't jump over the fact that Luke says some of the seed fell on good ground and produced crops one hundred fold. Even though the seeds that fell on the stony, thorny and hard grounds and those the birds carried away were lost, some seeds took root and produced a plentiful crop.

What can we learn from this? Hard work pays off. When you do the right thing, you can forget about the pains of your past, and you can glory in future successes. Keep goin'!

Look at Jesus' example. The next time we see Him after

He finishes teaching the parable of the sower, He's on the Sea of Galilee, and a storm blows up. He tells the storm, "Peace, be still," and it calms down. Then, after the storm, Jesus heals a man in a graveyard. Going through the storm was worth it because He healed a man on the other side.

Jesus faced difficulties, but He never gave up or gave in.

Then, after Jesus leaves the man, He runs into a huge crowd. Dealing with the masses is an inconvenience, but it's worth it because one woman believes in Christ, touches the hem of His garment and is healed.

Then, when Jesus finishes with the crowd, He ends up at Jairus's house. There are a bunch of doubters around, but it's worth dealing with them, because He is able to raise Jairus's daughter from the dead.

Do you see the trend? Jesus faced difficulties, but He never gave up or gave in. He kept going; therefore, there were great rewards.

Problems are part of the package. If you lose friends while helping others, it's all right, because God will never take more from you than He gives in return. It doesn't matter how many times your efforts seem to have gone to waste—keep sowing. The sower didn't give up just because some of the seed fell on hard land. He didn't decide to chill in the shade and wallow over his failures. He didn't throw his hands up in the air in defeat and exclaim, "I ain't sowin' no more! I'm done!" Instead, he persevered. He kept up the good work, and because he did, there were great rewards. By and by, serving the Lord *always* pays off, as according to His greater plan.

Jesus did the right thing, so we should too. He fulfilled His purpose—dying on an old, rugged cross, taking on our sin, snatching the sting from death and claiming victory over the grave. Now He's at the right hand of the Father—interceding for us so we can keep doing the right thing. Our "hope is built on nothing less than Jesus' blood and righteousness."

Accept Christ's promises of freedom and joy, and reclaim your peace. While you're moving through life and living for Him, don't stay silent. Tell others what the Lord has done and what He's going to do. Keep believing and keep sowing, and He will help you along the way.

Because of Christ's grace, we are empowered to keep doing the right thing. He has given us the ability to reach others for Him and to claim victory in our personal spiritual walks. No matter what the future may hold, Christ has given us *hope* for our journeys.

Discussion Questions:

1. Read the parallel accounts of the parable of the sower in Mark 4:1–20 and Matthew 13:1–23. When you read this parable, acknowledging that you're responsible to tell others about Christ, how does it alter your understanding of the different soils? What experiences have you had with each type of "soil"?

2. Why do you think Jesus outlined how difficult His road was going to be right after telling the disciples to follow Him? What might that same difficult call mean for your life?

3. What does Mark 4:14 mean when it says, "The sower soweth the word"? How can you better share God's Word?

4. What do you want most out of this life? Be honest. Maybe you want to succeed in a career, be an awesome parent or impress others with your knowledge. None of these are bad ambitions, but they can become detrimental when they take a place of precedence before God. What does it mean to find your identity as a follower of Christ?

Action Point: Throughout this book we've looked at several places where Jesus gives His followers hope for their journeys. I pray that you have been encouraged and that you can see how Christ sustains His disciples. Before going back to your busy life, pray about where you are in your spiritual walk, and ask Jesus to take you to the next level—no matter what that involves.

Learn to pray daily, love mercy, claim God's promises, and walk humbly with your Lord—the only One who can bring you through any storm and out of any valley. Jesus has an adventure waiting for you. Are you willing to walk with Him every step of the journey?

EPILOGUE

Now it's time to reflect on what you've learned throughout this book to make sure the message sticks. So let's take a little closer look at the truth we looked at in the introduction: we cannot overcome anything nor maintain hope for our journeys without the empowerment of the Holy Spirit.

In the fourteenth chapter of John, the disciples started pushing back against all Jesus' talk about His pending death. They didn't want to hear it. So in chapter 16 Jesus turned His language to talk about the cross and why He had to die, be buried and return to His Father. He says, "It's important for Me to leave you, because if I don't leave, the Comforter can't come. You need Him to come because He is going to be in you what I was with you."

Jesus knew that when He left to go to His Father, His disciples were going to need a helper to lead them in the right way. He explained something like, "Listen, guys, we've been hanging out for the last three years, and you haven't had to make too many decisions. If I went right, you went right. If I went left, you went left. All you had to do was watch and follow what I did, and you ended up in the right place. Now that I'm getting ready to leave you, the issues are going to get deep. You're going to need to know My voice without seeing

My body—so the Holy Spirit is going to come to lead you."

You need to be able to discern God's voice, because this world sends a lot of incorrect messages, and the Lord's truth doesn't blare at you from some heavenly loudspeaker. God speaks in a still small voice—declaring that He has a message and a purpose specifically for you. When you walk closely with Him, filled with His Spirit, God will help you see who is for you and who is against you. He will guide you in all knowledge and wisdom for an overcoming life. That said, the Holy Spirit speaks not in the flesh but in the spirit; so in order to benefit from His guidance, you have to tune your life to listen intently to Him.

So how do you know what God desires of you? How do you discern the Spirit's leading? Well, in addition to the Holy Spirit, God has given us His Word. The Bible is the external means by which we interpret the internal testimony of the Holy Spirit. In other words, when you think you're hearing from God's Spirit, you need to check what you think you're hearing with biblical precedent. Why? Because God is not going to tell you something that is not grounded in His Word.

You can trust the Word, because God does not make false promises. If He says He'll take care of you and protect you, then wherever He may lead you, He is bound by His word to watch over you. When you give the Lord control, He'll pick you up and set your feet on solid ground.

Why is God interested in bringing us out of our struggles? David says that He does it for His name's sake. He doesn't want His children looking like they have an absent Father. You can trust the leading of the Holy Spirit and God's Word, because His name is on the line. Even if you don't know what God is doing or how He's going to work out your situation, you can rely on Him.

In order to remain in God's care, all you need to do is follow where the Holy Spirit leads you. You just have to say, "Lord, I'm going to hold onto Your hand. I'll go wherever You tell me to go, whenever You tell me to go."

Just remember this: the Holy Spirit wants to comfort and direct you! In Him you have an ever-present affirmation of God's presence. With Him by your side, you have everything you need for a victorious journey. Amen!

This book was produced by CLC Publications. We hope it has been life-changing and has given you a fresh experience of God through the work of the Holy Spirit. CLC Publications is an outreach of CLC Ministries International, a global literature mission with work in over fifty countries. If you would like to know more about us or are interested in opportunities to serve with a faith mission, we invite you to contact us at:

CLC Ministries International
PO Box 1449
Fort Washington, PA 19034

———————

Phone: 215-542-1242
E-mail: orders@clcpublications.com
Website: www.clcpublications.com

DO YOU LOVE GOOD CHRISTIAN BOOKS?
Do you have a heart for worldwide missions?

You can receive a FREE subscription to
CLC's newsletter on global literature missions
Order by e-mail at:

clcworld@clcusa.org
Or fill in the coupon below and mail to:

PO Box 1449
Fort Washington, PA 19034

FREE *CLC WORLD* SUBSCRIPTION!

Name: _____

Address:_____

_____

Phone: _____ E-mail:_____

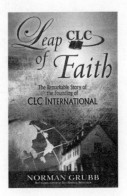

DR. ALYN E. WALLER

ENJOY YOUR JOURNEY

Our Quest for a Deeper Relationship with Christ

FOREWORD BY BISHOP WALTER SCOTT THOMAS

ENJOY YOUR JOURNEY

Dr. Alyn E. Waller

Life is more than a series of unrelated happenings. It is a journey, an exodus from sin and selfishness to the promised land of a deeper relationship with God. Join Pastor Alyn Waller as he follows in the footsteps of Moses and the children of Israel, in the journey of growth we all must take.

ISBN: 978-0-87508-824-2

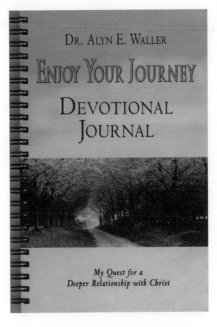

ENJOY YOUR JOURNEY

Devotional Journal

Dr. Alyn E. Waller

We all need to grow in our faith—applying the truths of God's Word to our Christian walks. Gleaning treasures from the Bible and Pastor Waller's *Enjoy Your Journey*, this devotional journal will help you remember the promises of God so you can mature in Him through every season of your life.

ISBN: 978-0-87508-893-8

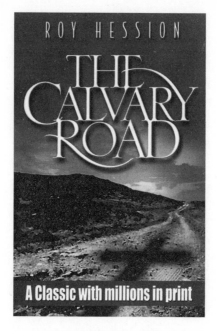

THE CALVARY ROAD

Roy Hession

Do you long for revival and power in your life? Learn how Jesus can fill you with His Spirit through brokenness, repentance and confession.

"This is one of the books that made the greatest impression on me as a young Christian, and in the work of Operation Mobilization around the world. We felt the message of this book was so important that it has been required reading for all who unite with us."

I would recommend every believer to read this book, and to follow up on it by reading *We Would See Jesus*.

George Verwer, Operation Mobilization

ISBN: 978-0-87508-236-3

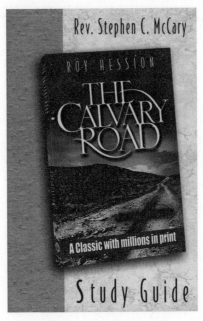

THE CALVARY ROAD STUDY GUIDE

Rev. Stephen McCary

A helpful guide to a timeless classic on the deeper life

This study guide is designed to be a chapter-by-chapter open discussion of the biblical truths taught in Roy Hession's classic volume on the crucified life. Stimulating questions, Scripture readings and fill-in-the-blank exercises will help you drive the meassage of *The Calvary Road* deep into your heart and life.

ISBN: 978-0-87508-784-9

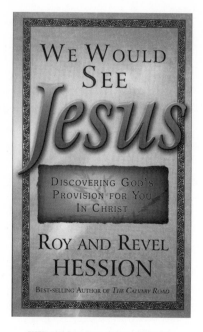

WE WOULD SEE JESUS

Roy Hession

Do you struggle with guilt or
feel like God can't accept you as you are?

It's easy to forget that nothing we do will make us more acceptable to God. Jesus came to set us free to serve Him in the freshness and spontaneity of the Spirit, and to receive the abundant blessing God has for us.

Let your life be transformed as you learn to see Jesus, who is both the blessing and the way to that blessing—the means *and* the end.

ISBN: 978-0-87508-586-9

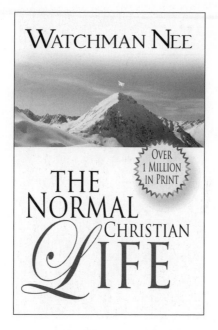

THE NORMAL CHRISTIAN LIFE

Watchman Nee

The Normal Christian Life is Watchman Nee's great Christian classic unfolding the central theme of "Christ Our Life." Nee reveals the secret of spiritual strength and vitality that should be the normal experience of every Christian.

Starting from certain key passages in Romans, he defines clearly and vividly the essential steps in the personal faith and walk of the believer. His emphasis on the cross and resurrection of Jesus Christ contains fresh spiritual insights that have proven a blessing to many.

ISBN: 978-0-87508-990-4

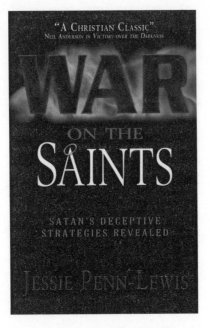

WAR ON THE SAINTS
Jessie Penn-Lewis

Has Satan got you fooled?

A witness of the Welsh Revival at the dawn of the 20th century, Jessie Penn-Lewis saw the rise of many extreme practices which brought about the decline of the spirit of revival. She, along with Welsh Revival leader Evan Roberts, wrote this masterpiece on such topics as "Satan and Demonism," "Counterfeits of the Divine," "Freedom for the Deceived" and more.

A valuable tool for all who seek to minister to both Christian and non-Christian alike.

ISBN: 978-0-87508-698-9